VICTORIAN DERBY

VICTORIAN DERBY

A portrait of life in a 19th-century manufacturing town

HARRY BUTTERTON

breedon **books**
PUBLISHING

First published in Great Britain in 2006 by

The Breedon Books Publishing Company Limited

Breedon House, 3 The Parker Centre,

Derby, DE21 4SZ.

ISBN 1 85983 533 3

Printed and bound by Cromwell, Trowbridge, Wiltshire.

Contents

Acknowledgements

The author wishes to record his sincere thanks to Trish Kenny and her staff at the Local Studies Library for their unfailing help and courtesy during the lengthy period of research for this book, and for making available the many contemporary photographs from their collection, acknowledged in the appropriate places. Also to Francine Smith, Sarah Allard and the staff of Derby Museum for their kind help in obtaining contemporary photographs from that collection and Picture the Past. Finally to my son Andrew Butterton for the many photographs of present-day Derby accompanying the text, also to Dr Frank Jones for several photographs that were taken for the *Derby Victorians* series.

Author's royalties from this book will be donated to the St Helen's House Trust.

To the senior citizens of Derby who

treasure their town

Introduction

The term 'Portrait' in the sub-title of this book should be taken by the reader in a decidedly impressionistic sense. If the author may be allowed in all humility to compare his work, purely of course for the purpose of explanation, to a canvas by the great Claude Monet, it represents a likeness of Derby in Victorian times done with daubs and broken outlines of local colour. It is his hope that it all adds up to a picture, however jigsaw-like, enhanced by the marvellous photographic images of the century before last, of life in the town at a particular time in something approaching its true and startling variety. To continue with the analogy with the visual arts the first section of the first chapter that follows might be likened to the picture frame or, crossing over to theatre, to the background setting before and among which the drama of everyday life was played. Only occasionally afterwards is there direct description of the buildings of Victorian Derby, the most immediate legacy of that age to us today. Because the people of Derby are the real subject of this book, not their works. The author's intention is somehow to take the reader back into an experience of the town as it was in the century before the last through the reporting in the *Derby Mercury*, its senior journal.

As regards the 'technical' details, the research necessary for the book is contained in the three volumes of my *Derby Victorians* series. This was based on the issues of the *Derby Mercury* newspaper in one year in every 10 during the reign of Queen Victoria. So words appearing within a pair of single inverted commas in the text of *Victorian Derby* are, unless otherwise stated, taken from the *Derby Mercury*. Indeed, each chapter opens with an extended quotation from that paper. One exception to this is where the *Mercury* itself quotes words actually written by correspondents (letter writers), taken from other papers or magazines or spoken, when the usual quotation marks are used. Explanatory words or phrases inserted into quotations from the *Mercury* within square brackets, thus [] are my own. The book is arranged in the usual topics or themes.

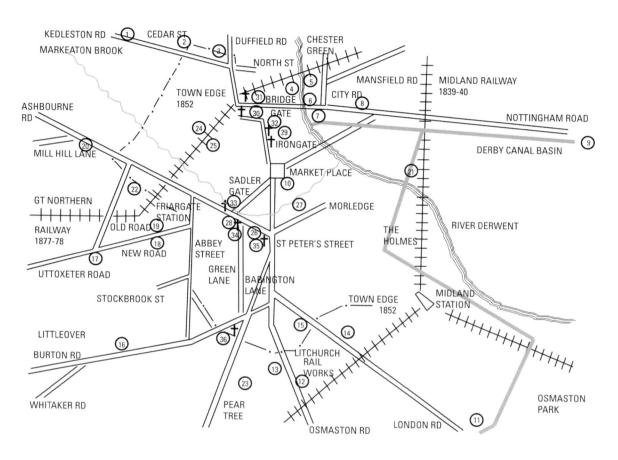

1	Parkfield Cedars	14	Litchurch Lodge	27	Albert Street
2	Parkfields House	15	Infirmary	28	Wardwick
3	Elms	16	Firs Villa	29	All Saints'
4	Britannia Foundry	17	Elmhurst	30	St Alkmund's
5	Union Mills	18	Cemetery (old)	31	St Mary's
6	St Mary's Bridge	19	Diocesan College	32	St Michael's
7	Phoenix Foundry	20	The Cedars	33	St Werburgh's
8	Convent	21	Long Bridge	34	Victoria Street
9	Cemetery	22	County Gaol		Congregational
10	Guildhall	23	Arboretum	35	St Peter's
11	Navigation Inn	24	Willow Row	36	Christ Church
12	Field House	25	Walker Lane		
13	Workhouse	26	Victoria Street		

CHAPTER 1

Unceasing Change

Angry writer to the *Derby Mercury* newspaper, October 1878:

> TOWN IMPROVEMENTS are capital affairs in their way; but we should scarcely apply this term to the paving experiments which, under the skilful superintendence of the Borough Surveyor, are going on in Friargate. From Stafford Street corner upwards, towards the bridge, the curbstones, laid down sufficiently well by the Great Northern Railway engineers when the road was lowered, have been meddled with and displaced until a series of very dangerous traps for foot passengers have been formed…

Do you grumble about road works, or streets carved up, or getting through cages of scaffolding, or balancing at the side of yawning trenches, or gazing over sudden acres of bulldozed space? Or having your ears split with a cacophony of drills and cranes and hammers all out to make a difference to a familiar corner of town you've known for years? Well, it could have been worse in Victorian times! Here's another sample, on a bigger scale, this time from the editor of the *Mercury* himself in January 1868:

> Considerable alarms were felt when it was proposed to widen Irongate, and to cut through the ugly block of buildings which separated the Corn-market from the Wardwick, and we were told that struggling tradesmen and professionals would be overwhelmed by rapidly increasing rates. Time has proved that these rumours were idle and unreliable. The great thoroughfare of the town – Irongate – has been widened without loss of convenience. This improvement will be pushed gradually, but surely, up to All Saints'. Through the Morledge a great advantage to those who use the Siddals Road will be obtained by the destruction of the Dusty Miller, and the expansion of the converging roads which lead to the new cattle market.

Iron Gate looking south, *c.*1859. Photo by Richard Keene before the street was widened in the 1860s when the shops on the left were demolished, to be gradually replaced in the 1870s to mid-1880s. (Courtesy: Derby Museums and Art Gallery)

What an upheaval it must have been, for all the editor's unflappability! The modern drills and bulldozers weren't there of course, or the JCBs, only picks, shovels, pulleys and hoists by the score transforming the Derby scene, going over the old streets in the middle, pushing up new blocks and towers, even domes, and adding whole districts out at the edges. Victorian builders made a huge difference to the old county town of Derbyshire.

But then, they just had to! When Victoria became Queen in 1837 there were about 30,000 Derbeians. When she left this world in 1901 there were over 100,000. Of course, their number has doubled again since then, but just think: Derby had been in existence for over a thousand years before the great queen came on the scene.

Filling the sky

It's the summer of 1837. You cross old St Mary's Bridge over the River Derwent to walk in the open fields on the opposite eastern bank and look back across at the town because it was nearly all on that side of the river. You may notice just a few buildings sticking up above the level of the packed house roofs. Taller than anything else, of course, is the tower of All Saints' Church, all 180 feet of it. To the right, the stubby towers of St Michael's and old St Alkmund's. Further to their right again the grim hulk of Rykneld Mills, now nearly 20 years old. Down at the riverside in front of the church towers, the century-old Silk Mill with its little new bell-tower. To the left of All Saints' the further stubs of St Peter's and brand new Holy Trinity and in front of them the slender dark finger of the Shot Tower, a mere 30 years old. Out of sight way back to the right of St Alkmund's, if not out of mind, lies the 10-year-old even grimmer County Gaol at the end of Vernon Street.

But the Victorians would soon set about fencing in the sky over the next 60-odd years, packing the space between river and horizon and beyond. They wasted no time. Here is a chronicle of their efforts to get the people of Derby to look up and around – and this is in addition to restoring or replacing most of those old towers, including glorious All Saints' itself and St Werburgh's, hidden behind it, in the 1840s and again in the 1890s, St Michael's in the 1850s and St Peter's in the 1890s. What effort, what energy! First, in 1838, St Mary's Roman Catholic Church went up, a splendid tower just to the right of old St Alkmund's as we're still looking across the Derwent. In 1839, Christ Church, Normanton Road, was built – a tower with spire on the horizon beyond All Saints'. In 1840 the Midland Railway Station block was erected, way to the left (and by the year 2000 long gone except for the clock). 1841 saw the building of the Royal Hotel and Athenaeum Club block right in the centre of town between All Saints' and St Peter's. In 1842, after a fire, the handsome Guildhall tower went up over the Market Place to the right of the Shot Tower and opposite the 50-year-old Assembly Rooms. Oh, and a conversion job just behind All Saints' took place to turn the Evans family mansion in St Mary's Gate into a chapel for the Baptists.

There was a breather till 1845, when the 'Crystal Palace' was built to help goings on in the new Arboretum way over the hill beyond Christ Church, and then a slight slackening of pace for the next few years. 1846 brought the brand new St Alkmund's, its tower and slender spire

Derby from the Nottingham Road, c.1860, a painting by H.L. Pratt. The Nottingham approach was still rural, though in the town mill chimneys regularly notate the urban profile. By this time the early Victorian splendours of St Mary's, St Alkmund's and the Guildhall have been added to All Saints' and the other old mediaeval church towers in the civic silhouette. (Courtesy: Derby Museums and Art Gallery)

(long gone, like the Shot Tower and the old Assembly Rooms) topping All Saints' at 200 feet after knocking the little old church down just to the left of St Mary's. By 1849 something is happening just behind us on this side of the river: the building of the Convent of the St Vincent de Paul (gone by 1863). And, more behind us back to the right, is St Paul's church tower overlooking Chester Green. In 1850, downriver to the left, a new bridge from the Market Place was built so that horses and carts could make a circle with the old St Mary's crossing. In 1851, on the horizon beyond St Alkmund's on the Uttoxeter New Road, a splendid red-brick pile for the Diocesan College for Training School Mistresses was erected overlooking the town cemetery. 1853 brought a new grand entrance to the Arboretum with a Roman-style statue of benefactor Joseph Strutt, and on Curzon Street behind All Saints' the Derby Temperance Hall, useful in the years to come for all sorts of occasions, was built. In 1855, another grand entrance on the far left horizon, this time to the new Nottingham Road Cemetery, took shape.

Another breather till 1860, then the construction of the Victoria Street Congregational Church – another tower and tall spire (gone too) near the centre of town behind All Saints'. In 1861 the Corn Exchange, dome topped with playful ball, was built just beyond the Guildhall. Also, way out of sight over the left horizon, red-brick towers and spires for suburban Methodists went up. Pause till 1866, then came the opening of the grand Market Hall between the Guildhall and the Corn Exchange after two years' construction. Meanwhile, desperate work went on in the space between All Saints' and the market, with the whole of the near (riverside) edge of Iron Gate coming down for road-widening as we've seen. 1869 saw the erection of the classy block of the General Post and Telegraph Office opposite the Victoria Street Church and, along to the right behind All Saints' tower, the Royal Drill Hall on Newland Street for the Sherwood Foresters (gone too). In 1870, far up Stockbrook Street on the horizon behind St Alkmund's, St Luke's Church with its high saddle-back tower was put up. And in 1872, St Anne's Church, with its tall bell-hood over Whitecross Street behind and to the right of St Mary's, followed. Just behind St Mary's a big new block, and later a chapel, was built for Derby School 10 years after moving into old St Helen's House.

Then comes another pause till 1876. Behind us on this eastern Derwent bank and to the right the mighty Haslams' Union Mills is opened, where ships' refridgerators will soon be first made, looking across the Green to St Paul's tower, now 25 years old. And beyond that, construction proceeds on the skeleton of the Great Northern Railway crossing of the river to tear through the northern suburbs of the town. In 1877, behind St Mary's, the gorgeous Friar Gate bridge carries the line on to completion and way beyond that on the horizon the Derby Union Workhouse (long gone) first casts its immense shadow over the lives of the poorest. In 1878 comes the Municipal Art School then Technical College, a marvellous Gothic pointy-styled block on Green Hill deep beyond All Saints', and down between them the luscious curve of the Strand is built for shopping. In 1879 the Free Library and Museum go up on the other side of the street, the splendid gift of Thomas Bass, the town's MP for 40 years, topped with yet another extravagant tower to back up All Saints'.

The building frenzy doesn't stop there! In 1881 there is a rebuild of the Derby Mechanics' Institution beside the Library, after 55 years, to be enlarged after another 13. In 1883, on the other side of the Library, the Art Gallery is built with more Bass generosity. And over to the

Derby College of Art on Green Lane, built in 1878 in flamboyant educational Gothic style. It became the Municipal Technical College after 1902. (Photo: Andrew Butterton)

right of St Mary's on the northern edge of town, the Derbyshire Hospital for Sick Children (recently gone) is built. In 1886, way to the left beyond the Midland Station, St Andrew's in Litchurch is constructed for railway families to worship in by the Liverpool Cathedral master of the pointy style Giles Gilbert Scott (long gone too). Also that year the Grand Theatre on Babington Lane behind St Peter's was built, which even had to be done twice over because of fire! In 1887, deep behind St Mary's off the Ashbourne Road, the massive Railway Servants' Orphanage (now gone) went up.

Yet another pause, and the frenzy continues unabated into the 1890s. 1891 sees the rebuild and enlargement of the 80-year-old Derbyshire Infirmary to the left of St Peter's, becoming Royal when Victoria herself came to open it. In 1893 the grandiose Poor Law Offices are built on 25-year-old Becket Street around the corner from the Drill Hall. 1895 sees the construction of the Midland Railway Institute, looking impressively across at the station itself, and to the right of All Saints' on Bold Lane the less impressive but spookily interesting Corporation service building for the welfare of the horses that pulled everything around the town was built.

In 1900, way beyond Christ Church and the Arboretum, the seemingly endless roll-call of Victorian church building projects in Derby came to a finish in Dairyhouse Road Methodist Church in bright red brick, though choosing not to add anything to the town skyline, certainly not if the viewer stuck to the riverside. Thinking about it, for whatever reason – Bible command, reverence for the unknown, moral values, social control – our Victorian ancestors do seem to have been obsessed with building churches, don't they?

But this was the ever-changing setting for the activities of Derby folk in Victorian times. Is any further proof necessary for claiming that Derby even in our time is still essentially a Victorian city, visually at least?

Nosing around

But what about at actual ground level? What did the Victorians do for the size or area of the place? Much the same story, really: horizontal expansion to fit in the tripling population. This is perhaps best shown by pushing along the main routes out of town in various directions and noting the changes that took place along them between 1852 and 1901, the years when the two best maps for the purpose were published. The first was the Board of Health map, the second the Ordnance Survey.

Of course, by the time the 1852 map was drawn the Queen had been at Buckingham Palace for 15 years already, so looking at it for signs of change is like scooping up water from the River Derwent, because houses and mills were constantly being added to the previous general map of Derby drawn in 1841. But the 1852 map was a quantum leap forward in accuracy and detail so we have to use it as our base-line for charting the difference the Victorians made to things.

Deciding to track westwards in 1852 and then move clockwise around the compass (please refer to the sketch-map near the front of this volume), we find ourselves clip-clopping along the Ashbourne Road out beyond the Wardwick, notebook ready. Look left... a glimpse of the gardens and fields that even this close in are just behind the buildings along the roadside!... only two gaps till just past the junction of the Old Uttoxeter Road, which at this date has no

St Alkmund's from Bridge Gate in about 1900. This was Henry Isaac Stephens's most important church building, built in 1846 in the almost inevitable Gothic style following the lead of Augustus Pugin, the architect of St Mary's directly opposite, on the site of an ancient Saxon and mediaeval church. It was demolished in 1967 to make way for the Inner Ring Road and it masked the view of St Mary's from Iron Gate. (Courtesy: Derby Local Studies Library)

hump of a Great Northern Railway bridge to get over in the near distance before climbing the hill up to the Burton Road… gap one just beyond the junction with Curzon Street – an uninterrupted view of gardens and fields… gap two at the junction with Vernon Street with the 30-year-old County Gaol scowling in the fields at the end… past Uttoxeter Old Road it's all open country with a few isolated villas like the Cedars breaking up the view… at that point it's the same on the right-hand side, though on that side right from the Wardwick there's a continuous fringe of buildings through stately Friar Gate (no railway bridge to go under yet!)… again snatches of gardens behind but closely backed up by humbler 'working' streets of mill-hands beyond.

Next, out from Iron Gate, trot along King Street… past the now six-year-old 'new' St Alkmund's steeple and St Mary's tower on the right… on into Duffield Road past the front garden of St Helen's House… newish terraces until the start of North Street going off east towards the river… now already it's open country with the Elms isolated at the fork with Kedleston Road going off front left… looking up the hill of Duffield Road a glimpse of the villas and gardens of Park Field and Grove Cottage… on the right-hand side of Kedleston Road is also open hillside… on the left a start has been made on terraced streets backed up at right angles by Parker Street with its Ragged School and Leyland Street… beyond Whitecross Street open land on this side too while further over St Anne's Church and the mills along the Markeaton Brook stick up over the edge of the Markeaton Hall estate.

Now back down Bridge Gate hill between those rival church towers on the right of lower Duffield Road… a few short terraces on the left behind the great Britannia Foundry on the side of the river… we cross by the old bridge as in 1837… two little sections of the town now on this east side of the Derwent… to the left a small triangle of terraces and mills then the three-year-old tower of St Paul's looking over entirely open country, save for a scattering of farms and houses, to the north where Chester Green will be formed later on… to the right, the Phoenix Foundry no doubt competing with the Britannia on the other side of the bridge for smoke and fumes, then the Convent of the St Vincent de Paul, designed by the great Pugin and only two years old and a fringe of housing overlooking the Canal… between that and the river the little colony of Exeter and Erasmus streets leading to the Long Bridge for canal barges to cross the Derwent downstream from Exeter Bridge… at the back of the Convent open country still… further out along the Nottingham Road one field between the last house and the mighty Midland Railway embankment making for Derby Station over the river… through the road arch under the line a glimpse of open Chaddesden Hill behind a row of canal-side works… way over to the left would be the Racecourse pavilion.

Now climbing St Peter's Street south from the Corn Market back in the centre of town… Babington Lane branches right before the fork of London and Osmaston Streets (Roads)… along London Street the Derbyshire General Infirmary in its spacious grounds on the right… a maze of terraced streets on the other side that lead to Siddals Lane beside the canal and the open Holmes meadow (within 20 years it will be the Bass Recreation Ground) beyond… to the right of that the station itself… just two long terraced Litchurch streets separating the Infirmary grounds and Osmaston deer park stretching towards little Alvaston… only Litchurch Lodge stuck out in space!

Back along Osmaston Street we find open gardens and fields just beyond Wilmot Street on the right and Bradshaw Street on the left... a block of terraces further on just before the Union Workhouse (the future Crown Derby works)... at the back of that is the Arboretum and the front looks across to distant Litchurch Lodge on the London Road... now it's all open country broken on the right by a series of villas, Field House, Ivy Cottage and so on.

Now we climb Green Lane from Victoria Street back in the centre towards Normanton Street (Road)... soon open fields on the left, and once we've got beyond the junction with Burton Road also on the right sloping down to the town centre... the views in that direction are broken up by a series of lead and silk mills... turn along Burton Road... no buildings after Mount Street apart from a series of villas on either side... Spa Lane on the right... that would lead us back down to Abbey Street with an almost continuous fringe of terraces with open fields behind on either side of the slope down from Burton Road towards the crumple of buildings in the town centre.

Finally, try the Uttoxeter New Road from below from Curzon Street... again it's a case of open hillside broken by a single brewery and some villas... on the right halfway up the red-brick fancies of the Diocesan Training College for School Mistresses look out on the white figures and stone wings of the 10-year-old town cemetery.

If we went back to the scene in 1901 to find out how much had changed, there would now be no gardens or fields along the Ashbourne Road until the junction with Mill Hill Lane. And if we were able to catch glimpses of what lay behind the house-border to left and right, there would be row upon row of terraces with an occasional mill block or gothic church or school tower rising among them towards the Burton and Kedleston roads.

If we happened to be rich enough we might now be behind an automobile bonnet rather than a horse as we trundled along Duffield Road. Looking down North Street on the right there would be a sea of brick dominated by the Children's Hospital with terraces sweeping right back towards Derby School and left over the former Strutt's Park. And in contrast to the case in Friar Gate leading to Ashbourne Road, we would have gone over rather than under the 20-year-old Great Northern Railway just past the entrance to the school. Forking left at the Elms on to Kedleston Road there would still be open land past Highfields Road on the right, belonging to Park Fields House and Parkfields Cedars, until we got to Cedar Street. We would then note the starts made on the terraces of Sherwin and Longford Streets. On the left there would be no gaps in the houses until a few yards back opposite Parkfields Cedars itself.

Down Bridge Gate to the other side of the river, to the left the terraces of Chester Green would have been added beyond the majestic front of Union Mills and the Recreation Ground with the Great Northern line running out from the cast-iron crossing of the Derwent. Between Mansfield Road and the Midland Railway to the east would be further terraced streets. In the other direction along Nottingham Road there would now be a fringe of mills and dwellings beyond the railway on either side right up to the cemetery entrance tower on Chaddesden Hill.

Making south along London Road there would now be no open land on either side between the Infirmary and the bridge over the railway, terraces to left and right, much more and deeper on the right side though St Andrew's would tower over the shorter streets to the left. Beyond the bridge there would be allotments for a while on that left side before the

The Morledge in Fairtime, 1882, a painting by C.T. Moore, a total contrast to Pratt's 1860 vision. We are immersed in the crowded townscape around the Shot Tower from early in the century, with mill chimney smoke very much a feature above the merrymakers. (Courtesy: Derby Museums and Art Gallery)

bulk of the Midland Railway's oil and grease store and past that would come another zone of terraces three deep but tapering further out to a squeeze between the road and the canal at the back separating the houses from the expanse of Osmaston Park. Just before the crossing of the canal would come the Navigation Inn and wharf for whatever boats still came this way. On the right-hand side of the road opposite the allotments would be a mass of rails and sheds between the London and Birmingham rail lines, but then open fields up to the canal and beyond, when the new terraces of Crewton would be reached. Here Brighton Road would curve round empty plots laid out ready for building on, to merge with Alvaston, while on the other side of the London Road it would be still open park country past the Navigation Inn.

Back on Osmaston Road again there would also still be open country beyond the Midland Railway works and Graham Street on the left. However, on the right there would have been massive building in the Rosehill, Pear Tree and Dale areas beyond the Arboretum.

Up Uttoxeter New Road we would pass villa after villa up to Elmhurst at the junction with the Old Road, where terraces would cover both sides of the hill back into town over the Great Northern line. Looking beyond the villas on the left more terraced streets would hem Stockbrook Street under the tower of St Luke's, reaching towards the ridge of Burton Road. If, finally, we had trotted this Burton route we would have found it continually built along, up to the Firs Villa and estate. Beyond that there would be fresh villa building along Whitaker Road, with Fairfield House and Littleover House further along on the left.

St Peter's Street 1858–9, photo by Keene. This side of the street was demolished for widening in the 1870s. At the bottom of the hill was Thorntree House, home of Joseph Strutt, where the garden featured the Florentine Boar before it was taken to the Arboretum after 1840. (Courtesy: Derby Museums and Art Gallery)

Shopping

> FAMILY DRAPERY. R. HIPWORTH takes this opportunity of gratefully acknowledging the kind patronage he has so long received from the Ladies of Derby and its vicinity, and which it will ever be his study to merit, by offering goods of STERLING VALUE, and the CHOICEST STYLES, adapted to a genteel and useful family trade. London House, 5, Irongate.
>
> *(Advert in the* Derby Mercury, *7 May 1856)*

While the Victorians might well be completely bemused were they able to see shop fronts shouting 'Toys R Us' or 'Computer World', we in turn, were we able to put the clock back sufficiently, might be astonished at the variety of trades carried on in streets like Sadler Gate in Victorian times. We would be exchanging a situation, at least in Iron Gate, where places to eat and drink in some style seem to predominate for one where, in Iron Gate again, there were 18 different kinds of trade or business carried on.

If we wish to take this further and get an idea both of the variety of businesses and trades in Derby in that period and also of how much change took place between earlier and late Victorian times, we should take a look at one of the trade directories for 1849 (Glover) and one for 1903 (Kelly – two years after Victoria died of course but, given the job of compiling information then, possibly as good as any for assessing the situation at the end of the century). If we look up three streets – Sadler Gate, Iron Gate and Bridge Gate, near the northern edge of town – we will find a mass of bare facts that will need some interpreting if we are to learn anything from them. For the full Directory lists for these streets please turn to the Appendix at the end of the book.

Of course we will have examined only three out of many shopping streets in Victorian Derby, so that for time and convenience's sake our picture of what went on will therefore be limited. But if our lifespan as a Derbeian had enabled us to experience these streets both in 1849 and, say, 1901, we would surely have at least mentally noted some interesting changes in those 50-odd years, just as we might do so now if we are able to compare the first two of these particular streets between 1956 and 2006. Bridge Gate, sadly perhaps though it must have been dirtily picturesque at best, is no longer with us.

Let's start with a simple head-count of businesses for each street for the two years. On Sadler Gate the number went from 26 to 52 (exactly double) and on Iron Gate from 15 to 46 (exactly triple), whereas on Bridge Gate there was a slight decline from 35 to 29. That's quite a difference! There was obviously a pull to the centre, the concentration of shops perhaps attracting further business starts. We can see this, perhaps, with butchers, confectioners, grocers and tailors in Sadler Gate, and architects, printers and especially solicitors in Iron Gate.

These details neatly show up the contrast in character between the two more central streets. Sadler Gate was definitely concerned with the more basic things of life, especially eating and drinking. Iron Gate was a sober, professional, definitely up-market zone, much more what we might describe as middle and upper class in an age notoriously concerned with class differences, and appropriate to Derby's status as the county town of Derbyshire since Iron Gate was the main entry point from the county itself. It had just one pub backed up by a wines and spirits shop as against the five on Sadler Gate. It did, however, have a restaurant and a tea and coffee shop, perhaps reflecting a feminine counter-move against pub culture which was most famously done in Glasgow where it provided a design opportunity for the great architect of the time, Charles Rennie Mackintosh.

Bridge Gate was obviously nearer the work face. After all, the Britannia and Phoenix Foundries would be belching smoke and fumes all day long at the bottom of the hill, one this side and the other the far side of the river. Apart from boiler makers there were makers of nails, needles, soda water and spa ornaments, though all these seem to have gone out of business or had moved elsewhere by 1903. Interestingly, the bang-up-to-date technology of travel seems to have been represented in Sadler Gate, with its cycle and car maker! However, there does seem to have been an explosive growth in grocers in Bridge Gate, including the Co-op, another Victorian creation from Lancashire, which had a store there, as it was presumably the daily shopping centre for the growing terrace area just to the north. There were also shoemakers to serve a hard-working mill population. In Bridge

Shop beneath the Shot Tower (right) in the Morledge, about 1900. The wall on the left belongs to a bridge over the Markeaton Brook before it joined the Derwent. (Courtesy: Derby Local Studies Library)

Gate, too, Sadler Gate's 'hairdresser-perfumier' becomes the humble 'haircutter' in the Directory.

Can we pick out any more general changes from all these facts, lists and statistics? Is it fanciful to detect a lessening of the connection between Derby as a county town and the countryside around as the suburbs pushed ever outwards? Does the disappearance, between our two reference dates, of the gardener/seedsman, maltster, milkseller and veterinary surgeon point to this, despite a farmer moving into Sadler Gate? There was surely more surplus money available to sustain the dining-rooms, confectioners and, especially, the extra architects and solicitors. The *Derby Mercury* records the first divorce cases in town and house-ownership was starting to increase. More basic still, the tripling population towards 1901 must have a connection with the multiplying butchers and grocers.

Can we also get some idea of how much change there was during these 50 or so years from the samples of a whole large town in these three particular streets? If we take first the 'professionals' such as accountants or architects, these increased from just six in 1849 to 16 in 1903. If we're talking about craft businesses, the number of these went up from 18 to 31 in 1903 (not such a proportionate increase). If services are looked at (including dining and drinking) these stayed roughly the same in number at 26 (roughly, because of the difficulty of differentiating 'service' from 'retail'). As regards retail itself, the number of this kind of concern went up from 10 in 1849 to 36 in 1903. Finally, in the manufacturing category there was actually a decrease in the number of businesses from five to three during this period, possibly due to this kind of activity moving out and away from the centre, though always just around the corner were the textile mills of north Derby. If we add up all the different kinds of concern, craft or business together for all three streets, we arrive at a total of 75 for 1849 and 125 for 1903. Taking into consideration the manufacturing figure and the fact that these three streets were old-established features actually in the centre or edge-of-centre of town and therefore unable to expand physically, we may see in these figures a reflection of the growth of Derby as a whole. The centre was catering in a servicing and retailing way for a much larger population living nearer the expanding edges (suburbs), where the manufacturing was mainly carried on and which were now connected to the middle by trams.

There is yet another way at looking at what went on, with a microscope. This would be looking at the trade directories for our two limiting years to find out how many firms or businesses with the same surname doing the same line of trade were still there in each of our three streets in 1903 from 1849. Excluding pubs, taking Sadler Gate first, out of a total of 45 named businesses in 1849 only two were still there in 1903, including Hart & Co., Chemists & Druggists. In Iron Gate, out of 42 named businesses in 1849 only one was left in 1903, namely Bemrose Stationers, Printers. In Bridge Gate, of 27 named businesses in 1849 none at all made it to 1903! Put another way, in our three chosen streets only three named businesses of a total of 114 survived the 54 years between our two chosen dates. Perhaps this is what we should expect over such a timespan of nearly an average individual lifetime. But it surely again goes to show that the Victorian age in Derby was one of great, possibly unnerving, change.

Whatever. Looking at it all from a different angle and from over a century later, what an amazing range of trades and occupations, ways of making a living or perhaps starting up the shaky ladder to comfort was represented in just these three streets.

Village Street, Normanton-by-Derby, looking east, 1889. This was one of the old village settlements surrounding the town which were being encroached on at that time by the expanding rows of 'suburban' terraced houses. (Courtesy: Derby Local Studies Library)

CHAPTER 2

Going Places

Darley Grove and its gardens have long since given way before the march of railway improvements; but it was quite a new sensation to find ourselves across Friar Gate and deposited by the train precisely on the spot where our boyish memories centre themselves on once smiling gardens, now the pathway of the iron horse.

(*Derby Mercury*, 24 January 1878)

Friar Gate Bridge, the spectacular crossing of the town's most elegant street to carry the GNR line into Friar Gate Station in 1878. (Photo: Andrew Butterton)

The *Mercury* reporter had been on board the inspection train that resulted in the opening of the Great Northern Railway line through Derby four days later. It was the fourth railway into town since Victoria became queen, but by far the most spectacular in the difference it made to the appearance of the town. The earlier lines had a clear pathway that did not involve the destruction of stuff in their way, merely crossing over river and canal. As we have already seen, the Great Northern meant tunnelling under or jumping over busy roads much nearer the centre of town. And in between those efforts and approaching them huge embankments dwarfed terrace streets on either side where they didn't actually engulf them, and archway following archway of dark brick stumped across the townscape.

While this was going on horse buses started up along Derby's streets, with the new Friar Gate station an obvious target as well as the old Midland on the other side of town. Three years later in 1880 they would be joined on the four big routes from the town centre, including this one along the Ashbourne Road, by horse trams trotting along ready-laid street rails. By this time the bicycle had arrived and would soon become a craze in personal transport. In another 20 years, by 1900, those who could afford it would have a motor car. Eventually, though not just yet, this would mean the final end of the age of the horse. The animal had been supreme when Victoria went to Buckingham Palace back in 1837, when the stagecoach was the thing for distance passengers and the horse-drawn barge on the Derby Canal for weighty goods. Though the first two railway lines reached the town from Nottingham and Birmingham just two years later and the mighty North Midland from Leeds only 12 months after that in 1840, how would you get from the station to anywhere else if not by horse-drawn vehicle of some kind? How would you move goods around in between if not by the carrier's waggon? The better-off, of course, would have their personalised two-to-four-seater conveyances and there were the horse-drawn cabs for hire up and down the town. In Derby the first threat to the supremacy of the horse away from the railway line would come just three years after the Queen's death, when in 1904 the electric tramcar appeared.

The kingdom for a horse!

In December 1900 the *Mercury* carried a story that possibly captures something of the clip-clopping magical sound-world of stagecoaching with the live backing of church belfries. When the coach from London arrived 'in olden times' there was an arrangement for church bells to be rung so that people who had ordered a delivery of fish might rush to get it as fresh as possible. It was said that the six bells of St Peter's, the first to be passed until 1836, would call out 'Here's fresh fish come to town! Here's fresh fish come to town!' Next came All Saints', further along that stretching main streetway in Derby, with a peal of 10 bells this time, 'Here's fresh fish come into the town! Here's fresh fish come into the town!' Just beyond All Saints' stood little St Michael's, with three bells only, and one of those cracked, and the sense of its peal was 'They're stinkin! They're stinkin!' But St Alkmund's with its six-pack a little further on again replied 'Put some salt on 'em, then! Put some salt on 'em, then!'

In reality the coaches stopped at inns and pubs. For example, in the 1830s at the Tiger and the King's Head in the Corn Market you could catch the *Defiance* and the *Bruce* for London, the *Standard* for Birmingham, the *Lord Nelson* for Manchester and the *Times* for Nottingham. But from 1840 they would fight a losing battle with the steam locomotive. Letters would be

The Cornmarket, illustrating the congested horse-drawn traffic of later Victorian times, with the possibility of harmful accidents. (Courtesy: Derby Museums and Art Gallery)

carried by stagecoach only where there was no railway, as in 1858 between Rowsley and Manchester according to Glover's *Directory of Derbyshire* for that year. If you had written to a relative in Manchester your letter would have gone by rail to Rowsley and then been transferred to the mail coach to go the rest of the way by road. And that arrangement wouldn't last for long either, as the engineers burrowed through the heart of the Peak towards Buxton.

However, the local roads would still be busy with animal power. And not just horses. In August 1837 the *Mercury* reported an accident to the London mail coach (rails were still two years into the future!). It had just passed over the canal on the outskirts of Derby when the horses took fright at a cart drawn by three dogs sprinting in the opposite direction. The horses jumped the hedge and the mail ended up in a field with the coachman and a passenger suffering broken legs. The reporter added that such dog-carts were becoming 'a very dangerous nuisance on turnpike roads'. In tragic fact, the coachman later died from his injury and the paper appealed to the generosity of its readers on behalf of his destitute widow.

Speeding horses seem to have been a bigger problem. The exit from Sadler Gate into the Market Place in the centre of town, with Iron Gate coming in down a slope from the left, was a danger point. In December 1837 a lady was knocked down and again suffered a broken leg at that spot. She was trying to get out of the way of a carriage emerging from Sadler Gate when she was hit by a 'fly' (horse-cab) being driven furiously down Iron Gate. The 'flyman' had determined to pass the carriage before it got in his way and Mrs Flack was caught by both horse and wheels. Another 30 years were to pass before the widening of Iron Gate and the demolition of this end of the Market Place could help solve the problem.

It wasn't only pedestrians who suffered. Horses could lay waste to property if not properly controlled. In December 1878 the *Mercury* reported that at about six on a Friday evening a cab horse, with its burden still attached and left on its own for a minute or two by its owner, walked into the window of a tobacconist on the corner of St James's Street. There was havoc! The window display was completely wrecked and the horse then walked away from the disaster with a sort of swagger, according to the reporter, who added: 'The shop was too small for a cab, or doubtless the vehicle would have appeared at the counter of the astonished attendant'.

And imagine what could happen if you lost control of your living, breathing engine on a really steep hill! Your speculation might possibly tally with what took place in Darley Abbey, then a hill mill village about a mile from the northernmost houses of Derby itself, in April 1846. The servant in charge of the horse pulling the four-wheeled carriage belonging to Mrs Douglas Fox, wife of the town's Medical Officer of Health, who was with her three youngest children and their nurse, lost control while dipping down into the village. The animal, said to be normally 'quiet and tractable', seemed to go berserk, plunging through streets crowded with workers leaving the mills. It first hit a wheelbarrow, throwing the eldest child on to the road where a rear wheel went over her head, then a post near the river's edge, causing the rest of the party to be ejected with severe cuts and bruises. The injured were taken first to houses in the village then to Darley Hall.

What a carry on!

As we have already touched on, what horse-power lost in distance travel when the railways came it gained in short hauls. Goods could arrive at speed at the station, or the nearest canal wharf if weight was more important than time, but that might still be far from where they were really needed. The gap was filled by the carrier with his horse-drawn waggon, the reason for a network of local routes until the early 20th century. The carrier was also the local passenger bus. Carrier routes were based on the town pubs. For example, from the still picturesque Dolphin in Queen Street, a carrier went on six days a week to Heanor, Langley Mill, Shipley, Stanley and West Hallam, on three days a week to Duffield, and on one day to Brailsford, Codnor, Ilkeston, Morley, Sawley and Stapleford (Glover: *History and Directory of Derby 1849*).

However, the carrier's waggon or cart could cause problems in the town's crowded horse-trafficked streets, especially if, like the Dolphin, a base pub had no parking such as was available, for example, at the Swan in St Peter's Street. In May 1867 cart parking was the subject of lengthy discussion by the Town Council. Aldermen Gisborne and Madeley moaned about the nuisance in Full Street and Victoria Street. The latter councillor thought that carriers' carts should be made to stand in the Market Place since no stalls were allowed there at that time and the tradesmen around were complaining about the consequent loss of business. However, Councillor Forman reminded his fellows of how essential carriers were to the trade of the town and pointed out that several inns would lose most of their business if carts were not to be allowed to be parked in the streets. The discussion was left at recording a

Rotten Row and Irongate, a painting by A.J. Keene based on a photograph he took in 1858. This scene would be totally altered a decade later with the demolition of the right-hand side. A carrier's cart is prominently parked in the foreground, predecessor of the later lorry and rural bus combined. (Courtesy: Derby Museums and Art Gallery)

plea to carriers and farmers not to place their carts 'in an obstructive manner' at pubs with no private space for the purpose.

This matter of parking was a long-standing problem, as a letter to the *Mercury* as far previously as December 1846 shows. The writer declared himself to be from the Wardwick Brewery and he related how the previous Friday he had sent a mule and cart round into Iron Gate to deliver ale. Though a second man stood by the mule while the business was proceeding, the driver collected a summons from 'the paid servants of our authorities'. The law on the subject, the writer thought, was about as clear as mud and was left to the 'inexperienced men' to interpret. The summons was in fact thrown out by the magistrates but the complainant still had to pay the costs involved, resulting, as he looked at it, in 'the regularly paid servants of the town' getting 'double salaries'!

Moving waters, perhaps

Though the superiority of rail was obvious when trying to work out a favourable ratio between weight of goods and time to supply or get them, even in 1858 the Grand Junction Canal, to which Derby's canal led, kept an office on Cockpit Hill advertising daily boats to and from a range of far-away places like London, Leamington, Leicester and Warwick (Glover's *Directory of Derby*). On two days a week boats went to and from Hull and Wolverhampton. Goods could also be carried by water to Burton, Rugeley, the Potteries, Manchester and Liverpool.

However, it was a case of slow decline, and by 1897 the canal, as its continued existence was reflected in the pages of the *Mercury*, appeared only as a possible, even probable, death-trap for children on holiday. A letter-writer from Derwent Row that summer claimed that scores of children had been saved from drowning at the 'dangerous locks near Meadow Road' and appealed to the Derby Canal Company to do something to prevent 'this summer terror of immersed children'. Ten weeks later a second letter from the same pen related that 'a little one was fished out in the locks near to the Long Bridge'. He mentioned two other recent young deaths in the canal, in addition to seven others luckily 'hauled out of the locks that dam the canal at Meadow Road Bridge, and the rescuers also damn the locks, too'!

Irresistible rail

From the time when, early in 1837, advertisements appeared in the *Mercury* on behalf of the Midland Counties Railway for contracts to supply bricks to be delivered during the summer for construction work between Nottingham and Derby, a new world had dawned. That summer the Birmingham and Junction Railway was also busy advertising work in Normanton and by the autumn near the Siddals Bridge over the canal. By the following summer the Derwent itself was ready to be leaped over. Meanwhile, the North Midland Railway, which would in the matter of a few years stage a takeover of the others, had already advertised a contract to 'make the Railway, with all the excavations, embankments commencing at or near Duffield Church… and terminating at or near the Turnpike Road from Derby to Mansfield in the parish of St Alkmund'. This meant that by 1840 Chesterfield, Sheffield and Leeds were wide-open destinations for Derby folk. As early as October 1838 the *Mercury* was crowing, awed by the spectacle of it all:

> Spectators cannot contemplate so prodigious a work without being struck with the conquest effected of mind over matter – the conversion of difficulties into facilities – the operations of thousands of individuals regulated by a few pervading minds – and the monument erected to human ingenuity and enterprise by a work so extensive, diversified, and beneficial.

In the 1840s Derby people who could afford it could taste the delights of the day excursion. For example, in September 1846 a trip went to Lincoln, leaving at eight in the morning and reaching the cathedral city at 10. While there were fewer aboard than expected, due perhaps, according to the reporter, to a gloomy morning and the Derby Races in a day or two, the 'far-famed Cathedral' and its 'celebrated choir' were duly appreciated. Exception was taken, however, to charges made by cathedral officials to see the 'various curiosities' there, such as a shilling to see King John's chair when 'twopence would have been plenty'. In July 1856 there was an excursion to Alton Towers, 'the Seat of the Right Hon., the Earl of Shrewsbury', to enjoy a 'choice Selection of Vocal and Instrumental Music' in the 'Ornamental Grounds' at 2pm. That summer, also, up to 10 special trains a day would leave for Matlock, visited by four to five hundred Derby people on a Saturday. One Thursday in August 'about 2,000 of well-dressed and orderly conducted people' went there 'under the auspices of the Derby Temperance Society'.

By 1867 Derby people were connected by rail to Liverpool via Crewe and Manchester, Bristol via Birmingham, Hull via Nottingham and Lincoln, Ashby via Burton, Rowsley via Matlock, Mansfield via Nottingham, Cambridge via Kettering, Ripley via Little Eaton, Rugeley via Birmingham and Wirksworth via Duffield. And all this was in addition to the great Leeds-Sheffield-London trackway.

The Midland account was not absolutely in the black. Judging by a brief passing obituary in the *Mercury* in February 1867, the station seemed to be a place where misdeeds might be expected, and the premises required the presence of an 'active, and obliging policeman in the booking-office'! Readers might sadly miss him in future as he had died the previous Saturday

The Midland Station by moonlight in about 1900. Outside is a horse-drawn tram, soon to be replaced by electric vehicles. The station had a classically-styled frontage designed by Francis Thompson, the Midland's architect. (Courtesy: Derby Museums and Art Gallery)

after a short illness, 'leaving a widow and eight young children totally unprovided for'. Biblical 'mites' were respectfully appealed for on her behalf. In August 1878 a correspondent signing himself 'A TRAVELLER' complained of the 'nasty coffee which a traveller must be very staunch to his temperance principles before he could swallow', served up in the refreshment rooms. He recommended for management's attention, instead, the coffee obtainable at 'the Friar Gate Cocoa House' at less than half the price of that at the station and which he declared was 'an infinitely superior and thoroughly palatable beverage'. Finally, in September 1897 another correspondent complained about the Midland service to Wirksworth as a daily sufferer, enduring up to 40 minutes' wait for the connection on to the Ecclesbourne valley line at Duffield for a train that took up to one hour 40 minutes to do the 14 miles to the terminus! This express mode seemed due to the custom of taking on the milk churns for market on the up-train instead of the more logical, to the correspondent, down-train.

By the 1880s Derby Midland Station was an enormous goods centre, as shown by the phenomenon known as Chaddesden Sidings, now part of Pride Park. A *Mercury* article in 1888 described how in this area 'goods traffic converges from every point of the compass, and is rearranged, made up into fresh trains, and again sent forward. Here a train arrives every seven and a half minutes throughout the 24 hours'. Shunting 'necks' opened out into no fewer than 35 separate lines on which to rearrange wagons. Six engines and up to 100 horses were constantly at work. It was fierce work, too, in cold weather when grease froze in the axle-boxes of trucks, often requiring three horses to pull a single truck. 'When to frost is added the yet more cruel impediment of a fog, the work becomes sometimes almost more than flesh and blood can stand.'

Northern strike

While all this was going on on the eastern edge of town, brooded over by Nottingham Road cemetery on its hill, over on the north and west another main line cleared whatever was in the way through 1877, as we have already seen in Chapter 1. By April 1878 the GNR was advertising a 'TRIP TO THE SEASIDE. DAY TRIP TO SKEGNESS BY THE NEW ROUTE'. Those tempted would leave Friar Gate station at 8.35am and return from 'Skeggy' at 5.15pm. Only the very poorest and the likes of the orphans for whom the Derby Seaside Home was founded in 1893 would be unable to benefit from a regular breath of liberating ozone from 'this time forth'!

One rail scheme for Derby failed to come about. In June 1888 the Town Council debated a proposal to run a light railway to Ashbourne. This would take the form of a 'cable tramway', though at least one councillor objected to such a plan because farmers along the route wanted a proper railway. The workers who might use it to come into town should be satisfied with a waggonette twice a week, though how this could possibly serve seems strange. Other councillors by contrast were decidedly in favour. A new line would attract country people into town and benefit the milk trade. But it disappeared from view – perhaps enough was enough looking back at the undoubted triumphs in and around Derby of the 'heavies' in the railway business. However, by the time this particular battle was being fought the horse had been groomed for a new kind of stardom, playing the part of an engine minus the steam, pulling coaches along rails in the middle of the streets.

The GNR bridge over the Derwent in 1878, originally with a pedestrian footway suspended below the main girders, constructed in the nearby Britannia Mills of Andrew Handyside. (Photo: Dr Frank Jones)

Trams ahoy!

For three years from 1877 horse-drawn omnibuses were the Derby street novelty providing transport from one part of the town to another for those who could not afford to hire a cab or own a 'convenience' themselves. Then in 1880, 11 years after their first appearance in England in Liverpool, trams took over from the horse-bus on four major routes, though not on the Kedleston and Uttoxeter Roads. They had to wait for another 25 years for the privilege and horses finally made way for electricity.

Trams didn't arrive without opposition of their own. A Councillor Russell claimed from countrywide travels that 'he did not know a single town with a similar population to Derby where there were tramways'. The inference was, of course, that they would be some kind of 'white elephant'. He reckoned people needed to travel at least two miles to work to make regular use of them. He was supported by the editor of the *Mercury*, who thought that trams would get in the way of trade in Derby's narrow streets 'by preventing the carriages of customers from drawing up at shop doors' (January 1878). There was no doubting the stratum of society that read the *Mercury*!

A horse-bus in Victoria Street in about 1880, with the Athenaeum Club behind and the porch of the Royal Hotel on the right. (Courtesy: Derby Museums and Art Gallery)

The critics were proved wrong. The Derby Tramway Company was a success story and the Council (Corporation) took it over 20 years later, again contrary to the free advice of the *Mercury*. However, in January 1900 the paper could legitimately criticise the Council over the excessive hours its 'tramway servants' were required to work. It claimed the Derby driver and conductor's day stretched from eight in the morning till at least 10.30 at night. This the *Mercury* likened to the life of a London bus driver, as reported by Punch some years back: 'Ho yus, hours is a most pleasant job; hi gets 'ome at midnight, and then 'as the rest of the hevenin to myself'. Nothing was done about it during the Queen's reign, the Tramways Committee even voting down by 21–8 the following July a proposal by Councillor Winter that trams be discontinued on Sundays so as to 'give their employees the same privilege of a Sabbath Day's rest as is accorded other employees of the Corporation'. Opposing, Alderman Duesbury claimed no fewer than 7,241 passengers had used the trams the previous Sunday. In August 1900 the Council went on to give the go ahead for the electrification and extension by over three times of the existing four miles of tramway, so ensuring at the very end of the century the final, if temporary in the long run, triumph of rail.

CHAPTER 3

On The Street

The year 1867 will be memorable in local history for the vast improvements which have taken place. Considerable alarms were felt, or were fictitiously pronounced, when it was proposed to widen Irongate, and to cut through the ugly block of buildings which separated the Cornmarket from the Wardwick, and we were told that the struggling tradesmen and professionals whose income is settled at a well-known immovable stage would be overwhelmed by rapidly increasing rates.

Time has proved that these rumours were idle and unreliable. The great thoroughfare of the town – the artery through which passes the main business of the trade – Irongate has been widened without loss of life, without loss of convenience, and without obstruction to business. This improvement will be pushed gradually, but surely, up to All Saints', where a capital view will be obtained to Victoria Street.

(*Derby Mercury* editorial, New Year's Day 1868)

As we have seen, Victorian Derby was endlessly on the move, and not just outside the railway stations. The Iron Gate affair was merely the most spectacular of the almost constant alterations and additions made to the overall street scene during the Queen's 64-year-long reign. Completion of a scheme could result in a street party, as in August 1837, the first summer of Victoria's Britain, when the covering over of the Markeaton Brook, from the bottom of St Peter's Street to where St James's Street would come out another 30 years later, was finished. The workmen and their families were treated to 'a dinner of good substantial fare including roast beef and plum pudding' under an awning set up on top of the covering arch. Sixty to 70 including the brass band sat down at three o'clock and at six over 100 wives and children were served tea and buns. 'Donkey races, swarming poles for hats, and other rustic amusements were actively carried on, to the delight and amusement of the younger portion of the spectators.'

Such schemes were the response to growing difficulty in simply getting through the place, so choked up with horse-drawn traffic was it becoming by 1860 at least. As we have seen with the Ashbourne Road, not every idea for alteration and improvement was given the go-ahead.

A public meeting in the Guildhall in February 1846 squashed a plan to drive a road through from the Market Place to the Midland station. It was supported by Douglas Fox, the Medical Officer. Siddals Lane, one half of the existing equation, was unfit to get cabs through 'because of the drays and wagons which were constantly going and returning from the various warehouses in it'.

In fact, it was inevitable that major alteration could not come quickly enough at times for people left high and dry by the tide of an expanding town. For instance, a correspondent signing him/herself 'CALIFORNIAN' wrote to the editor of the *Mercury* in September 1878 pleading with the Council to connect up Stockbrook Lane to Parliament Street and so to the upper end of Uttoxeter Road, the lack of which route was causing the locals a detour of a quarter of a mile. At the time there was a 'footpath running in front of St Luke's Church, and if this were widened into a good carriage road, it would be a great benefit to the whole district'.

Who's responsible?

Apart from the mess caused by construction and demolition, a perennial citizen's complaint then as now was the state of the pavements. In May 1837, before old King Billy (the Queen's uncle, William IV) was dead, a Mr Stevens was reported in the *Mercury* as complaining about the state of Sadler Gate, where from the Bell Inn down 'there was no less – for he had that morning taken the trouble to count them – than 58 broken flags, and many with holes in them'. At that time the owners of adjacent properties were responsible for the upkeep of the footway and maintenance depended on the town surveyor's promptness or otherwise in serving them notice to do so.

By October 1878 pavements had without question become the direct responsibility of the Council, which in the case of Friar Gate caused further problems for another correspondent to bleat about. He/she accused the Borough Surveyor of 'paving experiments', of not leaving well alone the recent work of the Great Northern Railway after lowering the road for it to be passed over by their magnificent bridge. The result had been 'a series of very dangerous traps' for foot passengers, which could very well appear as injury-compensation 'extras' in the local rates.

Far more worthy of complaint than broken paving was what pedestrian feet might get stuck in! On the evidence of a notice from the new Board of Health in January 1856, many householders were failing to place their 'ashes and vegetable refuse for removal by the Scavengers' on Wednesday and Saturday mornings in 'proper tubs and boxes', leaving distasteful piles of matter open to interference and spreading along the footway. It was not just a matter of what the eye could see but also of what the nose could smell. In September 1846 a letter in the *Mercury* complained of a 'very offensive and unwholesome smell' at the bottom of Iron Gate, of a decomposing fishy character. Pointing up the possibility of disease, the writer concluded: 'I can assure you, that a party of ladies (the other day) making purchases in a shop close by where the stench was so overpowering could not remain any longer for fear of being made ill. I was present at the time, so can bear my testimony to the truth of it.'

In the summer of 1878 waste disposal was still a major problem. A *Mercury* editorial in July that year, quoting *The Builder* magazine, backed up a claim that Derby ratepayers were

The Royal Hotel and Athenaeum Club (left), the focus of Derby's first town-planning project, completed in 1840. The Markeaton Brook was first covered over, burying the bridge at the bottom of old St Peter's Street. The foreground was the scene of a workers' party in August 1837. (Photo: Andrew Butterton)

getting a poor deal in the matter with dire consequences for the appearance of the streets. Householders might as required leave their refuse as tidily as humanly possible, but:

> ...the scavengers are too lazy to lift the boxes to the cart, so they tip them in the street, and then shovel and broom the filth in the usual way. Heaps of ashes, dust, pea-pods, paper, and the general miscellanea of household and culinary operations are left in the hot sun and blown hither and thither by the winds. The exposure for hours, waiting the irregular calls of the scavenger, is a great nuisance.

According to the paper, many householders were still tipping their rubbish in a heap on the pavement. In addition, 'there are the rubbish rakers, who make a point of investigating the contents of the "boxes", in search of stray valuables which will now and then find their way into these receptacles'. In April 1900 a *Mercury* correspondent with the signature 'A RATEPAYER' painted a final unflattering picture of one aspect of the Derby street experience that he/she claimed was far behind the times:

> Sir, – As I pen these lines, the Corporation dust cart is receiving my modicum of ashes, general debris, and waste paper. A fairly high wind is blowing, so, as the cart is already overflowing by at least two feet of its obnoxious contents, a great proportion of unpleasant material is scattered all over the place; into open doors, windows, gardens, and shops; in fact, everywhere but where it ought to be. And why? Because the authorities have set their faces against any covered conveyances. In most civilised towns, carts, similar in size and capacity to ours, are fitted with a thin corrugated iron covering, divided into four square lids, each with a handle affixed, by which it is opened to receive the dust, then shut down, and the cart moves on to the next house, and so on. In Derby, however, a little army of old gentlemen are employed to follow the carts with brooms to clear up the quite unnecessary mess. The situation amounts to a disgrace to the most rudimentary civilisation.

Inglorious mud!

Possibly even higher on the complainants' charter was the combination of evil weather and poor walking surface to create mud. In February 1856 a heartfelt plea to the *Mercury* editor from 'HOUSEMAID, 1,001 Gerard Street', urging him to 'just see what a mess we're in' – 12 inches of mud! She further declared, 'Take my word for it, there'll be something amiss. Some poor mortal will be getting stuck and lost', resulting in an exercise for the judgement of the Coroner. And in November 1878 another correspondent styled himself 'STICK-IN-THE-MUD' after protesting about the state of Bowyer Street.

In wintry weather of, course, the problem was at its worst, as yet another scribbler described graphically in December 1888:

> How blessed was the heavy shower of Thursday afternoon. For the first time for several days – I had almost said weeks – the footways and pavements of Derby were cleansed of their veneer of sticky mud, and one was able to walk upon them with pleasure, and not with that all-pervading sense of insecurity which makes one step very gingerly indeed in order to avoid slipping down full-length upon the nasty mess beneath. How many sweet feminine tempers have been ruffled this Christmas time by the discovery of several inches of black mud fastened on to the end of their skirts it would be impossible to say.

There were more organised deposits to contend with, temporarily at least, in certain streets. The Co-op contested an application by the Borough Council in December 1878 to force suppliers of coal to householders near the centre of town (in Sadler Gate for example) to deliver it in bags instead of simply off-loading it in bulk in the middle of the road, from where the customers would carry it in their own barrows. The Co-op argued that the coal was cheaper that way by 1s 6d per ton and this appealed to working-class customers, who were in the majority even in a street like Sadler Gate. The Guildhall hearing resulted in no decision. The case is certainly a reminder of the overwhelming importance of coal in life in Victorian Derby and also its downside – all those chimneys that needed sweeping and produced a nearly permanent pall of smoke over the town.

Urban livestock

There were other sorts of contributors to the state of the streets, some no doubt the source of impromptu amusement and excitement. There were all those horses of course, each animal producing, it has been calculated, three to four tons of droppings a year! The coming of the railway in 1838 made no difference to the variety of animal life to be found on the streets of the county town. In fact, it possibly increased the sheer numbers in connection with the cattle market and there could be danger as a result. In 1856 it seemed that Pamplona and its bull run had been transported from Spain to Derby. Due, according to the *Mercury* reporter, to 'the merciless manner in which they are beaten with thick sticks' through the utterly strange setting of urban streets, several droves of infuriated bulls galloped to and fro on their way to market. A couple got completely out of hand between there and the station and charged down Siddals Road, Canal Street and London Road 'overthrowing whatever came in their way, and seriously injuring several persons'. A boy was later tossed in the air, severely bruised and knocked unconscious, and a little girl was gored in the face. Both were taken to the Infirmary while other children had their clothes torn. The bulls were finally caught, one of them dragged in (to a truck) by the united strength of a number of men holding on by the horns, ears, and tail, and the ring in his nose!

As late as December 1897 two bulls found their way into a jeweller's shop on the Ashbourne Road. One was peaceable but the other reacted to confinement by charging the counter, moving it back nearly a foot, upsetting a tray of watches, knocking over five wall-clocks and pushing his head through the window for extra mayhem.

In June 1878 a 14-year-old boy from Arthur Street was killed by a cow in St Mary's Gate. It was being driven through the streets with others to market, suddenly 'became infuriate' and rushed at a number of boys, trapping them in an entry by the Probate Court. Sidney Kirk was pinned against the wall and trodden on. He was taken to the Infirmary very badly injured and died there.

Back in 1856 the owner of a wayward chicken which had got into St Peter's churchyard disturbed a hare. Sadly, this was immediately the subject of an impromptu hunt along St Peter's Street, Babington Lane, Green Lane and into Kensington, where the animal was struck and killed by 'a labouring man'. Obviously, the centre of Derby then was far nearer the country than today, despite the presence today of the 'urban fox'.

However varied the contributors to the street mess, there was sympathy, at least in some quarters, for the men who had to clean it up. From a letter to the *Mercury* in January 1897, signed 'WINDCUTTER', it would seem they had a raw deal in Derby:

Sir – I should like to be allowed, through the columns of your widely-read paper, to speak on behalf of men who perform for us a thankless and disagreeable work – our street sweepers. There they are, many past the vigour and prime of life, daily exposed to the rigour of our extremely variable climate, undergoing exposure and drenchings, often wet to the skin with absolutely no protection but what is afforded by their ordinary working garments.

Now, I ask our councillors or officials if it would not be better to provide some kind of rain-proof garments and so enable our sweepers to perform their work with some slight degree of comfort, besides considerably reducing the risk of numerous ailments which these constant drenchings must inevitably entail? Our soldiers, sailors, police, even the Corporation horses are equipped to withstand as far as possible our fickle weather, and it would be but an act of common humanity to provide oilskin sou'westers and capes and jackets for our extremely patient brothers.

Derby people also showed their appreciation of their street-servants in watching the annual 'Derby Corporation Horse Parade' as it wound its way around the main thoroughfares of the town on May Day 1900. After the giving out of £24-worth of prizes, contributed by councillors, for the best 'turn-outs' of carts and harness, at half-past twelve the procession, headed by the Fire Brigade, left their Ford Lane base for the plaudits of their fellow citizens.

The pot-hole challenge

In open country the so-called turnpike trusts had improved main road surfaces considerably since one-time Derbeian Erasmus Darwin had been driven to experiment in the science of carriage-springing by the desperate state of the roads around Lichfield in the 1760s. But things could be really bad a century later well inside a town like Derby. In October 1867 someone signing himself 'Q. CURTIUS' could protest to the editor of the *Mercury* about the 'shameful state' of the top end of Abbey Street, beyond the Belper Arms, where '20 or 30 yards of deep holes and bumps' caused traffic to make a long detour, unassisted of course by cones, and especially in wet weather.

That December a member of the Board of Health, Dr Taylor, spoke about 'the disgraceful state of Upper Gerard Street (yet again), as it was 'likely either to break your carriage or throw your horse down'. He put his finger on a major cause of discomfort which has endured ever since – gas and water companies putting down mains after the street surfaces had been laid down. 'As soon as ever a road was completed', he said, 'one or other of the companies commenced hacking it up'! The complaint was repeated in January 1878 in respect of the good doctor's home patch, Friar Gate, this time in the *Mercury* with a letter addressed directly to the secretary of the Waterworks:

My Dear Sir – The facts are these:- When the ground and road were excavated for the drains to my house in Friar Gate, I told the man to acquaint the Gas and Water Companies that the ground was open, and that they might lay their mains, and so save the ground being opened a second time.

In the evening when I found the ground filled up, I enquired what the Companies had said and done. The man Jackson told me he had been to the office of each Company, and they replied 'that they preferred opening the mains themselves independently, and would do so when required'. The Gas Company had since done work there but the Water Company not a thing.

The appliance of science

Until the early 19th century social occasions were timed to coincide with the full moon for ease of travel, as the name of the famous Lunar Society of Midlands Ideas-men in the later 1700s bears witness. In August 1837 a contract to light and clean the 212 oil lamps in the streets of Derby at that time mentions that the season during which they would be needed would end 'six nights before the Full Moon in May next'. But this wasn't nearly good enough for one complainant to the *Mercury* the following August, who asked why only a third of the said lamps were lit during the current pitch-dark nights 'when not the faintest ray of moonlight, and not a star was to be seen'. Not only that, but 'the dark corners, where light is most required, and lamps are purposely provided, are left in deep obscurity'. In April 1846, a member of the Council's Lamp and Road Committee reported that 'there was no lamp lighted between Mr Holmes' [carriage] manufactory [on London Road] and the railway station', a very busy part of town.

So there were faults in Derby's illumination scheme. By 1878, however, the 'magician Edison' was strutting his stuff in the States and in November that year a demonstration of the new phenomenon of electric light took place in Becket Street, directing the public's interest round the corner to the Drill Hall. Inside 'two electric candles placed on pyramidal pedestals' disappointed the *Mercury* reporter compared with the light outside. There was 'every now and then, a sudden variation of colour, or of intensity, caused probably by some unsteadiness of the

The Market Place before 1841, showing the giant gas lamp placed there over 10 years earlier to provide light at this focal point of the town. The front of the Guildhall in the background was destroyed by fire that year and was replaced by the present façade with tower. (Courtesy: Local Studies Library)

machinery used in producing the current'. The writer pronounced that the holders of gas shares needn't worry themselves and the *Mercury* also quoted a medical professor at a London hospital, in a letter to *The Times*, giving it as his opinion that while electric light might be great for the outdoors 'it can never be used as a room illuminant'!

The professor got it spectacularly wrong, though to be fair to him, in working-class homes, later council houses and so on, electricity was not universally applied until the 1940s, as the author knows from personal experience! But as regards street lighting in Derby, electricity was indeed ruling the roost by 1888. However, a *Mercury* report that September revealed a blunder in the Council's procedure. The new lampposts had been put up 'flush with the kerbstones', and so 'placing an obstruction in the way of cart wheels'. This meant that people were knocking the posts down and objecting to paying the damages. The Council simply had to replace damaged posts with ones set back from the kerb.

Naturally, the new mode of lighting was an attraction for the vandal. In January 1897 the *Mercury* reported a £25 reward 'offered for the discovery of the miscreant' who cut the electric wires in Derby. The result of his or her work was evident in Friar Gate, where there was to be seen in the dusky twilight the figure of a Corporation workman earnestly beating the iron column of a lamp which would not burn with both hands in the apparent hope that the jar would set the light going. Failing that, he unlocked the door and inspected the machinery, still without success, and for the rest of the evening the lamp was useless.

Electricity was now applied in yet another way, as in November 1888 a new telephone exchange run by the National Telephone Company Ltd was opened at the Lecture Hall in the Wardwick in Derby, to rival the existing Post Office system. According to the *Mercury* report the general manager from Birmingham promised subscribers would soon 'be able to speak straight through to London firms'. As regards the effect on the street scene, to accompanying laughter he remarked that he 'failed to get people to see that a telephone pole in a garden was an ornament'!

Those nuisances

Animals, as we have seen, could be a pain as well as a pleasure in the street, but there were other sources of annoyance, too. There were smells. We have already met with the 'pestiferous and dangerous malaria' or, more realistically, fishy smell at the bottom of Iron Gate in September 1846, which was so bad that ladies had to abandon their shopping. There must have been many other spots offensive to the nose, possibly including the riverside where, that same summer, the Derwent was being used as a dump, according to the Mayor. The narrower Markeaton Brook was much worse. Upstream from the bridge at the bottom of Sadler Gate it was reported at a Council meeting that the Brook was a 'depository for filth and dead cats and dogs'. The gas works on the bank sometimes let out an 'impure liquid' that smelled badly. But more widespread would be the pong from badly-drained houses, from 'untrapped gullies', channels that never led anywhere. The Medical Officer in 1846, Douglas Fox, reported that of 1,050 such gullies in the town only about 60 were connected up to the drainage system. The problem was that it was a householder responsibility only.

Smoke must have been a problem too. Paintings done near the end of the century by A.J. Keene, now in the Goodey Collection in the Museum and Art Gallery, show a Derby which

Work-a-day Derby, a painting by A.J. Keene in 1905. The scene is from a back window on North Parade near St Mary's, illustrating the smoke-palled cheek-by-jowl interlocking of terraces and mills at the end of the 19th century. (Courtesy: Derby Museums and Art Gallery)

is spiked with tall factory chimneys belching out plumes of dark smoke. A *Mercury* correspondent signing him/herself 'A RATEPAYER' in August 1878 complained about it and implied an adverse effect upon health. The letter ended: 'I, with many others of the ratepayers of the town, cannot afford, or have not the means, of enjoying a sojourn at the seaside, and by that way get our lungs and blood purified of all its pernicious and carbonaceous impurities, but am obliged to remain at home and breathe the impurities complained of'.

That same summer another writer complained about the cacophony of noise in Derby streets. He or she claimed it was bad for anyone trying to do brain-work with any sort of deadline in mind. Particularly obnoxious to this individual was the noise produced by the organ grinder, bad news for anyone of a nervous disposition or possessing 'an ear for music'. There was also an accordian player in the Corn Market who 'pumps forth the melodies of MOODY and SANKEY [very popular hymn tunes of the time] with the most annoying persistence'. Then there were, of course, the 'screaming news-boys' bawling 'Hevening Noos!' in one's ear, in addition to the 'German band (with instruments out-of-tune and a badly-braced drum, beaten out-of-time)'!

Presumably the 'musical' performances in whatever mode were put on with the expectation of some financial reward. The records of the Borough Police Court tell us that there were many who attempted to persuade the Derby man or woman in the street to part with their money without the benefit of a performance. In December 1878 two 'very little boys, whose heads were on a level with the top of the dock' were accused of stopping a lady, one on either side of her, in the Market Place the previous day and asking for money. Their parents had

The Corn Market in about 1900, when accordian players, German bands and the cries of newspaper boys were sources of 'noise pollution' to the squeamish. (Courtesy: Derby Local Studies Library)

been in trouble previously for not sending them to school. The lads were ordered by the Bench to be sent to an Industrial School.

Drunkenness was a problem, then as now, and was the subject of complaint by a *Mercury* correspondent in September 1838. The writer lived in King Street and was appalled by the fact that no policeman appeared on the scene when for 'nearly two hours' after midnight a 'tremendous uproar' was kept up outside a beer shop there. His bedroom resounded with the noise of 'heavy blows and falls, and horrid blasphemy and vociferous obscenity'. When he finally opened his window and offered 'a considerable sum' to anyone who would fetch a policeman he was met with abuse 'disgusting in the extreme'.

Despite the writer's message, drunkenness was probably the most frequently charged offence at the Borough Police Court. At the beginning of the Victorian period there were about 127 hotels, taverns and pubs in Derby's streets, with an additional 42 retailers of beer. There were nearly twice this total by 1901. Female offenders featured in the Court's annals alongside the men. In February 1856 Mary McDonald, a 62-year-old Scotswoman, was let off after being drunk the previous Saturday afternoon in Queen Street when she undertook to 'gang awa to Sheffield in the morning and be seen in Derby nae maer'. In July that year two teenage girls were charged with being drunk, shouting and 'using very improper language at one in the morning in the Market Place'. A lady named Mary Ann Ford, a 'well-known personage', repeatedly tried the Bench's patience with successive appearances for drunken disturbance of the peace the same month, first at three in the morning in the Corn Market, then at 2.30am in the Willow Road, shouting and kicking the arresting officer, Constable

Dakin, in the leg. The men were of course far from innocent. In January 1867 a man was twice guilty of drunken early morning brawling in the same road.

More serious, if possibly less obnoxious, was a spate of stone and other missile throwing in the streets in September 1846, which caused injury to several women. During the same month hoop-trundling was said to be putting the lives of people on horseback and in cabs at hazard. Boys were in the middle of another craze in October 1867 by snapping pocket pistols in people's faces, especially women. During the more severe winters of the Victorian age, Derby street pavements were made extra hazardous by children making slides. This was reported in December 1846 with an appeal to householders from the *Mercury* to keep the pathway in front of their properties clear of snow and ice by sprinkling salt and then sweeping. The danger had not passed 10 years later when an elderly lady was reported as having fallen on a slide and fractured her thigh.

Characters

However, street people could be attractive too. In April 1888 the *Mercury* featured an article about some old characters whom it suggested would be sorely missed in the future Derby street scene. There was 'Daddy', who had died the previous year at the Union Workhouse on Uttoxeter Road after no less than 40 years of wandering about the town 'seeking shelter where and how he could', in receipt of the occasional coin, 'tottering along as was his wont, with his little basket in one hand, and in the other an oaken stick, which aided his gait, and

The Piazzas in the Market Place, demolished in 1870. It was a fine spot to listen to the cries of street traders. (Courtesy: Derby Museums and Art Gallery)

seemed the man's only companion'. He would 'shake his shaggy face at every passer-by', was hardly ever bullied by the street urchins, and with native cunning knew exactly where to call when desperate before finally, in old age, having to seek the shelter of the workhouse. And there was old 'Salt-O', who made the Market Place ring with his cry 'Fine leather laces, a penny a pair' and old Jerry, the pie man, who prided himself in 'his neat little cottage and favourite parrot'. Finally, there was the old gingerbread man, without whom the writer declared no Arboretum Day was complete. He charmed the Princess of Wales (later Queen Alexandra) when she visited Derby in the 1880s with his presentation of a packet of his gingerbread 'done up in a white satin wrapper', being rewarded with 'one of her most winning smiles'!

Gone shopping again!

Shops in town must have attracted people from a distance, then as now. Iron Gate would have been the first port of call for the ladies of the various country houses around Derby, such as Markeaton Hall or Meynell Langley, when chasing the latest fashions. In November 1837 Mrs Salt at 22 Iron Gate advertised the fact that 'her sister is returned from London' with 'an elegant Selection of fancy Millinery, in Caps, Bonnets, Cloaks, Ribbons, Artificial Flowers, with every novelty in Ladies Attire suitable for the Winter Season'. However, such ladies might well by that time of year not have had to use the family coach for the distance from their out-of-town residences. Until the coming of the Midland Railway and its express route to London just a few years later, many of them would have enjoyed the privilege of a family Derby town house as a base from which to enjoy the winter season's delights, such as the Hunt Ball at the Assembly Rooms. In June 1846 Mrs Hipworth at No.5 repeated the trade manoeuvre for the forthcoming summer. In April 1856 she appeared to be concentrating on 'Dress-Caps, Head-Dresses, Mantles', in competition with J. Haskew's at No.2, who claimed 'The Largest, the Cheapest, and the Best Stock of Bonnets'.

There were of course rivals in other locations. There was John Steer, 4 Market Head, who advertised in April 1846 as 'Umbrella and Parasol Maker', who 'respectfully informs the Ladies of DERBY and its Vicinity, that he has prepared a much larger STOCK of PARASOLS, for the present, than for any preceding Season, and which is now ready for their inspection'. In March 1856 Mrs Hall and Co. advertised her new shop at 61½ London Street specialising in corsets, especially a patent number worn by 'Her Most Gracious Majesty the Queen'. Finally, in November 1856 Edward Holmes at Cavendish House, 40 Corn Market, was now 'showing a Choice Selection of FURS, from the least expensive to the most costly in Sables, Ermine, Minerva, Squirrel, Musquash, &c., &c., and of the best Manufacture, at such prices as must give satisfaction to every Purchaser'. This was in addition to his 'LARGE STOCK of VELVET and CLOTH MANTLES, JACKETS, and OPERA CLOAKS'.

The matter of half-day closure

Derby shoppers in 1901 would find that quite a number of their favourite haunts would not be open one afternoon each week. It took a long time indeed for this essentially humanitarian situation to come about. In December 1856 a meeting of the town's Retail Traders in the Grand Jury Room of the Guildhall on a Monday evening agreed on a resolution, after much

General groceries store at 47–51 Leman Street, still going in the 1970s, the shop of first call in a working neighbourhood. (Courtesy: Derby Local Studies Library)

discussion, to the effect that 'the time of closing of the retail shops in Derby be not later than half-past seven o'clock during the five summer months, except that on Thursday evening the grocers and provision dealers close at eight o'clock'. This surely goes to show the general business feeling that faced a new Early Closing Association formed just a week earlier in the same building. This group declared a different philosophy, that the prevailing long business hours were 'unnecessary for public convenience, incompatible with the interests of employers, and injurious to the welfare of Assistants'. One speaker, draper Mr Beswick, at the traders' meeting, attended incidentally by 50 to 60 people according to the *Mercury* reporter present, in effect admitted that the retail trade had been left behind on this issue by the town's manufacturers. He maintained that 'factory operatives' generally shopped for his line of goods on Saturday afternoons, 'the mills generally closing on that day at 2 o'clock'.

The 'open all hours' ethos was just the same in 1867 as regards shops, judging from a letter to the editor of the *Mercury* in October that year, though it had obviously 'moved on' for others. The writer, Mr H. Steer again, a jeweller of 4 Market Head, urged retailers to join, in the summer months at least, with bankers, professional men, manufacturers, mill-hands, carpenters, bricklayers and many other workmen, close at two o'clock and have a half-holiday on Saturday. This would give more time for cricket, rowing, and outdoor exercise, and enable many more to take advantage of the special trains. To many a hard-worked employer, as well as to his wife and family, the boon would be great; and would tend to better observance of Sunday. Mr Steer was still fighting the good fight in 1878 when he spoke strongly in its support at a well-attended meeting of 'male assistants and apprentices in retail shops' in November, again at the Guildhall, chaired by the Mayor himself. Steer stated that his health 'had been most severely tried by many years of long indoor business', supporting a letter to the *Mercury* the previous May that declared it was not only drapers 'who do not close until half-past seven from 8am or earlier!, and even then the assistants do not get out until eight, and sometimes half-past, which leaves no time to spend either at home or elsewhere'. Steer maintained that half-day closing worked well in London, Manchester, Stoke 'and numerous other places'.

The proprietor of the new Cocoa House in Friar Gate gave his employees a half-holiday a week and 'the company gained by it. He did not know one man or woman connected with that establishment who did not work more cheerfully.' The Mayor concluded the meeting by urging a general acceptance of this view. The editor of the *Mercury* backed him up, though he considered the Mayor's added advice to shop assistants to spend their hoped for free time in sitting at home to 'improve their intellects' rather idealistic. Such a plan would 'appear to be about the last thought that enters the minds of the bulk of our young people; and the result is that our streets are filled with saunterers of the semi-swell assistant class, or loungers of the altogether low and blackguard type, to the inconvenience and annoyance of decent foot-passengers'.

However, even by February 1888, unlike the case in most other towns, according to a *Mercury* correspondent signing him or herself 'Grocer's assistant', shops closing early one day a week were the exception in Derby. The writer noted that one 'leading provision merchant in the Market Place has commenced to close'. Shop assistants were not helped by the town's two so-called 'Liberal' MPs that May when they both helped to defeat an Early Closing Bill in Parliament. Early closure was obviously not universal even in 1897, when, in October, a *Mercury* correspondent urged shoppers not to buy anything after 7.30 in the evening or, indeed, at any time from a business that didn't close on Wednesday afternoons on the strength of a personal experience:

> I was greatly astonished when walking down the Normanton Road on Saturday to find drapery establishments open and in full swing at eleven o'clock at night, and the same shops mark you, were also open on the Saturday afternoon. I went into one (not to purchase) and was told by a pale, tired girl, these were 'the winter hours', winter hours forsooth! Evidently a tradesman's term for 'sweating'. These poor girls are beyond the help of the law, (the masters know this and inflict whatever hours they choose) and their emancipation must come from the hands of the public.

Something old, something new

Whenever you did your shopping some street space would very likely have been occupied by the taxis of the age, the horse cabs or so-called hackney coaches. We have seen already how, recklessly driven, they could be dangerous. According to a complaint to the *Mercury* in November 1846 this essential mode of private hired transport was not as well organised in Derby in early Victorian times as it evidently was in neighbouring towns like Nottingham and Leicester. It was only after that date that designated stands for cabs or coaches, with appropriate fare scales, came into operation. This step forward was immediately followed by service advertisements in the *Mercury* such as the following:

The Market Place in about 1877, with a stand for carriages and cabs. (Courtesy: Derby Museums and Art Gallery)

GEORGE HAYNES begs to inform the Gentry, Clergy, and Inhabitants of Derby generally, that he intends to COMMENCE with a FLY STAND in DERBY, on MONDAY NEXT, and he hopes to have good HORSES, and careful Drivers, and by strict attention to the comforts of all parties employing him, to merit a share of public patronage. Orders received at Mr.J.BASSENDINE'S, Victoria Street.

Forty years later the pedestrian had to cope with a novel form of personal transport that in the 1880s became a craze, a means of liberation for women even more than men. The bicycle hit the street, and indeed the dusty county road system beyond the borough. In the town it led to a controversy that keeps coming back to haunt us to this day – should the cyclist be forced to sport a bell to warn the pedestrian of the machine's approach? On the evidence of a *Mercury* correspondent in September 1878 the 'jay-walker' was abundantly on the scene then. A cycle-bell would hardly save this specimen of urban humanity:

In crossing a street some people will walk across as if there were no danger at all. They never look round to see if any vehicle is approaching, and seem to expect that all traffic should be suspended till they have crossed, forgetting that neither a carriage nor a bicycle can stop at a moment's notice. There is doubtless truth in this, and when bicyclists voluntarily adopt proper precautions to prevent accidents they ought to have fair play on our streets.

And 20 years later, something really revolutionary, though for a few years yet fairly rare, appeared for the pedestrian to cope with – the motor car. In November 1897 a motorist escaped with a warning from a charge of 'Furious Driving' at the Borough Police Court. He denied the allegation of a police constable that he drove 'very fast – at least 12 miles an hour' up the crowded Duffield Road. A key part of his defence was that 'children were following all the way', therefore he could hardly have been guilty of such demonic pace!

Something special

In May 1900 the automobile provided a special occasion for the Derby street scene when 58 cars taking part in the Automobile Club's 1,000-mile test passed through the town en route from breakfast served at Lichfield for lunch at Matlock Bath. As far as the newspaper reporting of the event was concerned, interest was largely animal-focused rather than mechanical or technical:

> The Derby dog is a perennial feature of the great race at Epsom, but he has brothers of equal inquistiveness at the town of Derby. Your provincial cur has not yet learnt to differentiate between a cycle and a motor; but he is in process of being educated this week. He finds that he can worry a cyclist, but a motor car – well, he finds nothing at all, for he dies an obstacle in the path of progress, and this with all the good will in the world on the part of the driver.

The streets of the town had surely known more pronounced special occasions in their long Victorian experience, performances that must have fostered a sense of community as opposed to the show-off individuality of a motor rally. Though perhaps displaying a narrower straight-laced ethos than most of us might care for today, there were the annual May Temperance

The former Temperance Hall in Curzon Street, the starting point for May Day processions from the 1850s. (Photo: Andrew Butterton)

Festivals when hundreds of children accompanied by bands processed their way from the sponsors' Curzon Street Hall through the main streets to the Arboretum. The 1856 occasion was played an evil trick by the weather, for when the park was reached 'the rain descended heartily, and continuing with scarcely any intermission throughout the remainder of the day, the party who had assembled were obliged to seek refuge in the lodges, refreshment and other tents.'

In May 1856 too, the week after the Temperance Day, came the celebrations to mark the end of the Crimean War. The streets echoed to the thud of a cannonade as early as four o'clock in the morning, a Wednesday, to be succeeded by the clang of the bells of the five parish churches in the centre. Shops were closed, flags and banners 'waved profusely', garlands crossed overhead and houses were festooned with 'evergreens and floral wreathes'. Nearly 9,000 Sunday School scholars marched from the Market Place with two to three hundred banners, accompanied by members of Friendly Societies and factory workers. There were even photographers to record the scene.

The summer of 1867 also saw two special happenings to activate Derby street life. In June, a civic procession wound its way from the Guildhall to the Holmes meadow by the river to

Stand for the Golden Jubilee Procession for Queen Victoria in 1887, in front of the Royal Hotel. (Courtesy: Derby Museums and Art Gallery)

mark the opening of the Bass Recreation Ground, presented to the town by its senior MP Thomas Bass. In August a party of 25 Belgian Volunteer soldiers arrived at the station to march 'through a dense and somewhat disorderly crowd' to an official reception at the Market Place as the guests of the Derby Volunteers. There 'the house-tops were fringed with courageous climbers, and from every window ladies waved their handkerchiefs'.

Probably the most memorable street occasion during later Victorian times was the two-day celebration of the Queen's Diamond Jubilee in June 1897. As had happened 10 years previously for the Queen's Golden Jubilee, 'leading tradesmen and many householders' put out the flags and bunting. Not just in the main streets: the *Mercury* reported that 'in some districts the humblest cottages were resplendent with the national colours – the red, white, and blue'. A big crowd was attracted to the Market Place on the Monday evening to see the Guildhall illuminations and till past midnight 'the town presented a gay and animated appearance'. Three thousand electric lamps produced a sight 'by far the grandest ever seen in Derby'. On the sunny Tuesday crowds paraded up and down the main streets from early in the morning, many people wearing 'hat bands of red, white, and blue, and others had rosettes in their buttonholes, of the same colour'. Trams and other vehicles were also bright with flags and bunting. In King Street 'suspended across the road near the Old Flower Pot was a garland with a flag at the centre which was unfurled at the Coronation. On the Duffield Road the Derby School [St Helen's House] was covered with flags and shields and bunting.' Across the river in the afternoon on Chester Green 6,000 'delighted children' sang out the National Anthem with vigour in the presence of the Mayor before the inevitable evening bonfires at various recreation grounds, lit when rockets were fired from the Shot Tower in the Morledge. There was a charitable postscript on the Wednesday befitting a town where one of the mills beside that same Green had brought out the first refrigeration equipment for steamships. At the Drill Hall in Newland Street 'over 500 poor persons' were given a share of meat donated by 'the Pastoral and Shipping Interests of Australia' at seven in the morning, 'in accordance with the lists sent in by ministers of religion and through other agencies'.

CHAPTER 4

At Home

LOT 1. A CLOSE OF RICH MEADOW LAND, called WEST PARK FIELD CLOSE, situated a short distance Northwards of the KEDLESTON ROAD, in the parish of St Alkmund, containing nearly Three Acres, together with all TITHES OF HAY arising therefrom. This Lot is delightfully situated ON A GENTLE EMINENCE WITH A SOUTHERN ASPECT, about one mile from Derby, and a quarter of a mile north of Kedleston Road, from which there is an excellent PRIVATE CARRIAGE WAY, with a LODGE ENTRANCE; and presents a MOST ELIGIBLE and UNRIVALLED SITE for the erection of A MAGNIFICENT FAMILY MANSION, with appropriate Offices; and the formation of GARDENS and PLEASURE GROUNDS THERETO.

The beauty and privacy of the situation cannot be surpassed by any in the neighbourhood. It is removed from the annoyance of any public road, and commands EXTENSIVE VIEWS of the surrounding delightful Country. It is richly ornamented with handsome TIMBER, and is effectually sheltered from the North and North-east winds by stately old Trees. The Proprietor of a MANSION on this Elysian spot would have advantages which but few enjoy; and to a Gentleman seeking quiet and serenity, this offers a RETREAT such as is often sought for, but seldom found.

(Derby Mercury 29 July 1846)

Was this indeed paradise? It would be another 50 years and more after this surely tempting piece of estate-agentese before the Kedleston Road would become an area of denser settlement for townspeople with far humbler expectations than the advertisement's theoretical target. The rising ground on the north side of this important route out towards the beauties of Kedleston Hall still has sufficient greenery left for us to recognise that it could once have been as Messrs. Moody and Newbold the auctioneers described it more than a century and a half ago.

While the great bulk of the domestic building in Derby during the Victorian age consisted of rows of sometimes elegant terraced houses, for the workers of all kinds necessary to its destiny as a flourishing manufacturing centre, there were privileged pockets of real estate that might appeal to the individuals who had achieved success in life. For instance, advertised in April 1846 there was:

THAT excellent and commodious FAMILY RESIDENCE, called 'THE ELMS', situated at the junction of the Duffield and Kedleston Roads, within a short distance of the town of Derby, having good Stabling, Carriage house, large Walled Garden, and every other requisite convenience, now in the occupation of Henry Whitgreave, Esquire, together with a GENTEEL DWELLING HOUSE, adjoining thereto, with Stable, Garden, &c., in the occupation of the Revd E.H. Armitage.

In February 1856, in the street that today reminds us the most insistently of the even earlier and more elegant Georgian age, on the market was:

No.84, Friar Gate, Derby, containing dining, drawing, and breakfast rooms, two kitchens, laundry, butler's pantry, seven bed rooms, and four dressing rooms, water closet; good cellaring; garden, two-stalled stable, coach-house and other out offices, now in the occupation of Mr Holmes [boss of Derby's prestigious carriage works].

And positively top of the range must have been the home that was up for auction in February 1888:

ALL that excellent Freehold FAMILY RESIDENCE, known as 'The Cedars', Littleover Hill, Derby, comprising entrance hall laid with Minton tiles, 34ft by 8ft, 3 reception rooms, handsome billiard-room, lofty and spacious kitchen, scullery, butler's pantry, lavatory, and other domestic offices; beautifully-designed conservatory, floor laid with Minton tiles 35ft by 25ft 6ins., with large fountain in centre and plate-glass folding doors opening to breakfast-room, servants' bedchambers with second staircase, excellent wine and beer cellars &c... The Residence is built of red brick with massive carved Hopton stone ornamental dressings, entrance steps and portico of Hopton stone. The conservatory and billiard-room are of modern design, with bell tower. The Property is situate in an elevated position, and being tastefully laid out regardless of cost, is undoubtedly one of the most imposing Properties recently offered.

Another planet?

While the skilled worker, the office clerk and the 'lower rung' salaried professional might expect to be able to afford to rent or even own a decently-appointed terraced or 'palisaded' (with tiny fenced front garden) house in one of the many new streets going up in a wide arc stretching from the north round to the west and south of the town centre, there was a problem for those who could not expect regular work. Their number was such that this difficulty was never remotely solved in Victorian times. A sizeable proportion of Derby's population must have been classed as poor. Since the idea of the 'council house' was not acted upon on a national basis until after World War One (1914–18), though as we shall see it was 'in the air' long before then, this class of people would still be able to afford to rent property, mainly from landlords who themselves could not or would not afford to keep it in a decent state of repair. The Conservative Government at Westminster in the 1870s was well aware that this was a national problem and put an Act through Parliament encouraging local authorities to do something about it. The first step was reporting on the actual state of housing 'artizans' or workers had to put up with.

Court No.3, off King Street, a painting by A.J. Keene, illustrating the living space of a fair proportion of Derby's poorer people, in confined courts sometimes behind a front of business premises. (Courtesy: Derby Museums and Art Gallery)

And so while those with salaries, and perhaps able to employ a 'maid of all work' to ease the burden of the housewife, might think of moving into tree-lined Hartington Street, an investment of the powerful Woodiwiss family in the 1870s, the editor of the *Mercury* commented in December 1878 on the horrors of daily life for the poor of the town, which were revealed in the inquiry into the situation in Derby in response to the Act:

> Filthy rookeries and disgraceful dens were found to exist, in which human beings struggled hopelessly to lead clean and decent lives; whilst in other cases men, women, and children were huddled together in brutal disregard of all the decencies of life. And all the time we had been flattering ourselves that Derby was not as other towns in this respect.

The worst area for housing was the Walker Lane and Willow Road district just beyond the end of Bold Lane to the north of the town centre. The report considered that the only solution to its problems was to knock it all down and start again. Among the many black marks the surveyors noted 'the general lowness of the rooms, and the narrow cramped stairs, with an entire absence of provision for ventilation.' Then there was the severe overcrowding caused by sub-division of 'the once large gardens and roomy courts' to put up small tenements 'occupied by the lowest and most depraved of the community'. The result was simply to 'foster and encourage a low vitality, squalor, immorality, and vice'. Walker Lane among other horrors featured 'a row of tall buildings, presenting the appearance of their having withstood a siege'; also 'twelve privies… in a nest back to back, seven feet from a dwelling, all in a tumble-down

St Mary's RC Presbytery, home of the redoubtable Revd (later Monsignor) A. McKenna, champion of the poor. (Photo: Andrew Butterton)

condition'. Excrement and urine were everywhere. In Willow Row one house had a gutter running through a bedroom and the door of another had to be kept open at all times because of the stench from a privy immediately beneath the fireplace.

The Act's solution for this kind of situation presented a further problem: it also ordered proper provision for the unfortunate people displaced through demolition within the same area or at least nearby. The Roman Catholic priest at St Mary's just around the corner, the Revd A. McKenna, who peppered the *Mercury* with letters on the subject, asked how the Council was going to deal with the 2,700 folk he estimated would be affected. And the problem wasn't confined to the central area. Back in April 1867 another *Mercury* correspondent blotted Alvaston's copybook as 'a desirable place of residence on the southern edge of Derby' with the news that 'many families are at present living in houses ill-contrived, unhealthy, and overcrowded'. The consequence was that 'during the whole of last summer a slow typhoid fever prevailed, which has lingered in some houses through the winter, and there are indications of a threatened outbreak with increased virulence at the present time'. The writer went on to give supporting detail: 'A father, mother, and six children sleep in one room – the only one – of one poor cottage. In another cottage that the occupants have decorated with flowers, the father, mother, two young men, and a daughter have but one bedroom of a few feet square'. And so on with further equally challenging examples. The context and cause of the evil in Alvaston was also laid bare: 'Several of these houses have privies within a yard or two of the house-door. Most of them were built without any regard to sanitary requirements, and have never been improved. They are chiefly occupied, not by agricultural labourers, but by the employees of the Midland Railway Company…'. Obviously, not everyone shared in the Company's gift of prosperity to the town.

Old Alvaston, scene of a sanitary scandal in 1867, when the church designed by Derby architect Henry Isaac Stephens was just over 10 years old, having replaced an older building. (Courtesy: Derby Local Studies Library)

The dire housing situation in Derby was still there in 1897 when the Medical Officer, Dr Iliffe, was quoted in the *Mercury* as saying that there were hundreds of dwellings 'which are unfit to live in' and recommended the Council step in and remedy things directly by providing cheap houses. Only the Council, 'able to borrow on cheap terms, could afford to put up houses which could be let at the cheap rates required'. By November 1900 the Revd McKenna could compliment the authority on real progress in this matter but was critical of the design of the new dwellings being put up, pin-pointing the consequences: 'Few of them are properly lighted, and people have to grope their way up and down them; in most of them there is no handrail, and in nearly all of them the rise in each step is about eight inches or more. Only the poor have to put up with stairs of this kind. A week seldom passes without accidents to aged people on these abominable staircases. People in passing quickly from the kitchen, say, to the scullery, often injure themselves through momentary forgetfulness of the step down'.

Those chimneys!

Earlier in Victorian times another design fault had bitter consequences for many of the male children of the poorest families. John Claudius Loudon, a Scots-born designer who had a huge influence on the appearance of parks and houses and, as the creator of the Arboretum opened in 1840, is remembered in the name of Loudon Street nearby, advised builders to make a feature of proud tall chimney stacks. The trouble was that they had to be cleaned and maintained and many had a bend in them that made it convenient for them to be swept by hand. The hands involved were those of young 'climbing boys' small enough to crawl up the narrow vertical and twisting passages with brushes, scraping tender knees in doing so. Householders were summonsed for allowing their chimneys to catch fire through not being regularly swept.

The *Mercury* newspaper from 1837 carried on a 20-year-long campaign to stop master sweeps employing climbing boys and instead adopt a machine that was doing the job in London as advertised in December that year. The trouble was that, to start with, only four Londoners could be trusted to work it properly and 'will punctually attend orders by the twopenny post; charging exactly the same prices as those paid to the common chimney-sweeper'. This was hardly likely to please desperate customers and was also guaranteed to antagonise the local master sweeps.

However, there was a local committee to further the cause and promote local machine operators, one of whom was a William Roberts of Willow Row! He proved to be much less successful than John Jepson of St Peter's Street, who by August that year had managed to become the sole official operator. In the same month the *Mercury* reported one 'builder of eminence in this town' declare that he would never construct another chimney 'which could not easily be swept by the machine'. At the same time some owners of awkward chimneys were inserting a new iron-door device that could enable the machine to be used on them. The paper declared: 'We shall be much surprised if they who once give the machine a faithful trial ever employ climbing boys again.' In September it was reporting: 'During the last week, 103 chimnies (sic) have been swept by the society ['For Superceding Climbing Boys']'s agents.'

Nevertheless, even as late as 1856 the Society was having to prosecute master sweeps for sending boys up chimneys. Three years previously the Mayor (Alderman Madeley) issued an order 'to call upon all the master sweeps and prevail upon them to discontinue the practice', according to the Society's inspector, and they had signed up. But still there were 20 boys being employed in the town for this foul work. One pathetic case featured nine-year-old Robert William Littlewood, the illegitimate son of a Leicester single-mother factory worker who had hired him out at 20s for the year to a Derby master named Capenhurst. Capenhurst relieved the lad of owners' penny or halfpenny tips, struck him and forced him up 'as many as twelve chimneys in one morning' and so 'had injured the cap of his knee'. Robert did admit that his master had bought him a cap and 'he had a penny every Saturday night'. Capenhurst also claimed he saved his wages for him at the request of the mother. He got off with a reprimand.

Despite the example of men like T.W. Evans of Allestree Hall, chair of a meeting at the Guildhall in December 1856 to bring about the end of such practices in Derby and whose father had installed 'about half a dozen iron doors' in the Hall's flues, the town was lagging behind Nottingham, Birmingham and Leicester, let alone London, where there were no climbing boys left. The meeting heard that in Leicester poor master sweeps had had machines bought for them. The sweeps had to be won over but the end was nigh for this shameful episode in the history of household maintenance, even in Derby.

Dire poverty

There were many who could hardly have afforded the attentions of a master sweep with or without a machine. What sort of home had James Annable come from, the subject of a *Mercury* Borough Police Court report in December 1867? 'James Annable, a dirty half-starved little boy of eleven, was charged with stealing three oranges from the stall of Mary Baker, in the Market-hall, that morning.' Inspector Fearn said 'he believed the lad was much neglected'. One of the magistrates thought he looked 'half-starved', though his step-mother claimed he had 'plenty of food when he was at home'. Detective Stibey said the boy had been 'in the habit of standing in the Market-hall [just finished the previous year] from morning till night, and if the people there gave him nothing to eat he had nothing; he had also been in a state of almost nakedness'. The boy himself said 'his mother did not give him something to eat every day', though she claimed 'her husband had had no work for some time, and they only had a shilling or two of her own earnings to live on for some days'. Since the boy's head appeared 'diseased', the Bench 'thought a doctor had better see him'. When the Inspector said that the boy's brother looked even worse this lad was brought in and looked 'as much neglected as the other, and very filthy'. After a lot of thought the magistrates decided the lad would be better off in gaol for the next three weeks as at least he would get food and attention there.

A *Mercury* report of another Borough Police Court case in June 1888 enabled a closer look at a possibly similar home background: 'Annie Pool, aged 9, was charged with begging in Ford Street on Wednesday night. The girl, who was in a most neglected state, went to the house of Police-constable Fullerton, begging, saying that her mother had been dead seven years, and that she had no food. The officer instituted enquiry, and it seemed that she lived in St Michael's Lane, the house being very dirty, and no bedding, the children having to lie on rags. The father was found in a neighbouring public-house, drinking with some companions. The policeman added that it was the dirtiest house he had ever been in, the place containing several dogs and puppies, the stench being unendurable. The Bench sent the child to an Industrial School till she was 16 years of age.'

The Poor Law Guardians' offices in Becket Street, as rebuilt in the 1890s in Continental style. The Borough Education Offices were directly opposite. (Photo: Andrew Butterton)

By that time community help for those unable to cope on their own had for over 50 years been given either at home or in the institution called the Workhouse. This was the creation of an Act of Parliament in 1834, just a little earlier than Victoria's coming to the throne. The Workhouse was to be run by a committee of so-called Guardians, who were the representatives of the ratepayers of a district called a Union. It was meant to be the last-ditch refuge for those who were able to work but could not obtain enough of it to support themselves or their family. 'Out-door relief' could be provided for the sick or chronically ill in their own homes. However, the Poor Law relief figures for Derby, as for many places across the North of England, show that far more people were indeed helped in their own homes than through the expensive Workhouse. This was probably due to common sense and sympathy. The *Mercury* reported in April 1837 that the Board of Guardians of the Derby Union had discussed the rule of the Poor Law Commissioners (in far away Westminster) 'forbidding relief to the able-bodied poor in their own homes'. No decision was made that week 'but it appeared to be the general feeling that the regulation could not be enforced, at a period of such general distress as at present'.

The background to this discussion had been reported in the *Mercury* the previous month (March 1837):

> It is known to the public generally that the past Winter has been one of peculiar suffering and privation among the lower classes of society [very similar terms were to be used in the *Mercury* to describe the situation in 1905–06, early on in the reign of the Great Queen's son!]; this has arisen from a scarcity of employment, from the remarkable severity of the weather, and from an almost unparalleled amount of personal affliction. From these combined and powerful causes scenes of distress have occurred in this Town and Neighbourhood, such as those only who have witnessed them could believe to have existed. Whole families have been without any of the necessities of life, without food or fire, or anything that could bear the name of either clothing or bed linen.

'... and the greatest of these is charity'

A Benevolent Society had been formed in the town to provide charitable help at a time when trade was bad in the aftermath of the bitter silk mill dispute of 1833–4 and before the establishment of the rail industry in Derby in the 1840s. The *Mercury* reported what the Society's members found when setting out to see the extent of distress and need:

> William Taylor, Waterloo street, is nearly blind, has no parish settlement, has a wife and children to support by collecting rags and bones, seldom earns more than 6s. a week, and frequently not more than 3s. On being visited the family was found in most desperate condition, with very scanty clothing, and nothing but straw to lie on. Mary Welch aged 27, resided in Court 5, Walker Lane, with two young children; was found in great want of food and clothing, and, to all appearance near the point of death for want of necessary food, of which she had not partaken for two or three days. George Parfield, residing in Baker's-Buildings, London Road, has a wife and 5 children; was very ill and unable to work, had no coat, being a stranger in the town, and no friendly help. Two chairs, two or three small stools, a table, a large box, and but one bed, composed his furniture. The whole weekly income was but 2s. Being an Irishman he had no parish. Having but one pair of shoes his wife and himself were obliged to wear them alternately.

The Liversage Charity Almshouses on London Road. The Charity was the source of much help for the surrounding poor people of St Peter's parish in hard times. (Photo: Andrew Butterton)

At Christmas 1855, the old Liversage Charity in the Parish of St Peter's provided 'blankets, flannel, and calico, coals &c.' for 211 families and for 232 families the following Christmas. The combination of severe winter weather and unemployment as a direct result of it or the effect of economic depression would continue to make demands on the charitably disposed in the town, as a letter from a Sister Katherine at the St Anne's Mission House published in the *Mercury* in February 1888 makes clear:

> Dear Sir – Will you allow me to plead through your paper the needs of our Mission House, and the sick poor in our parish. I need hardly say that the present severe weather has caused much sickness and distress in our midst and in consequence we are quite unable to meet the demands on our resources that are made for the sick much less the starving. I shall be grateful for money for coals; meat for beef-tea, eggs, jam, clothes of all kinds.

There was also the time-honoured soup kitchen to provide basic sustenance, as reported in the *Mercury* back in February 1838:

> The Poor of Derby having been much distressed during the last year in consequence of the great scarcity of employment, especially among the framework-knitters, and the late inclement season having thrown many labourers out of work, it has been judged highly necessary to provide them with good Soup at a reduced price twice a week… Subscription books are left in all the bankers and booksellers in Derby.

The same sort of initiative was needed and produced in later Victorian times in the form of 'Robin Dinners'. One of these, the idea of a Miss Buckland of Measham Villas on the Ashbourne Road, was recorded in the *Mercury*, this time in February 1888, when 300 children were given 'a hearty meal of excellent soup and bread' in the Congregational Schoolroom, London Road, on a Wednesday, to be repeated at the same time each week into the spring. The largesse did come with a price-tag attached: 'The cravings of hunger having been satisfied, a practical scriptural address, adapted to the intellectual capacity of the gathering, is delivered by one or more of the clergy and ministers of the town, after which the children are dismissed'. By 1893 it had been succeeded by a Robin Christmas Dinner Society which gave 'a substantial meal of Old English Fare' at the Drill Hall each year to nearly four thousand children, according to the *Mercury*. The reporter noted: 'Upwards of two hundred ladies and gentlemen volunteered to assist in serving the children'. However, the Society also continued to dispense soup and bread, for example the 'one thousand gallons of soup, and three hundred stones [14lb x 300] of bread distributed by it during the severe weather of 1895...'

At the workhouse

Because of the absence of the social security net invented in the 20th century, hard times for those who could not afford the subscription to a Friendly Society could mean that their final home was the Union Workhouse. The stark consequence for so many was spelled out by a critic of the system, the Derby MP J.G.B. Ponsonby, at a meeting in April 1837 and reported by the *Mercury*: 'Decay of trade, or a broken limb – either of which might deprive the poor man at a moment's warning of the power to earn a daily subsistence – met with no other reward than a home broken up, and a separation of wife, husband, and children, when assistance was requested'.

Some rebelled against the regime, as in the case of Emma Wombell, referred to in the *Mercury* in September 1867 as 'a refractory and destructive pauper'. She was charged at County Hall (St Mary's Gate) with 'having broken 87 panes of glass at the Union Workhouse, Litchurch', which was a separate authority from Derby until the 1870s. The rampage had followed a 'petty' disciplinary episode: 'The porter at the Workhouse said that on Sunday morning at breakfast time the prisoner was talking in the dining-hall; the master told her to be quiet, but she continued to talk, and he again requested her to leave off; the prisoner replied that she should talk, and told the master to leave the hall'. However, the authorities did attempt to make life pleasanter from time to time, even if with what we might now regard as an excessively patronising tone. In September 1867 the *Mercury* reported a Mr Draycott getting the Derby Board of Guardians to allow 'a few of the old people in the workhouse... to sit or walk in front of the house on one or two days a week. Mr Draycott said it would be an acceptable little change for the old people, but he would give them to understand that the privilege was liable to be withdrawn if the order of the master against communicating with persons outside was not strictly complied with.' The most famous of jollier perennial workhouse episodes was, of course, on Christmas Day, when, as again in 1867 at the Union building on the site of the present Crown Derby works, 'an excellent dinner of roast-beef and plum-pudding' was served to 200 inmates and to another 100 ill or infirm in their wards. Children got nuts, oranges and toys donated by generous individuals. At the later workhouse in Markeaton parish (which later became the City Hospital) 'ale and tobacco was freely circulating' at Christmas 1878 according to the *Mercury*. In January 1897 'an excellent magic lantern entertainment was given to the inmates of the above union in the large dining hall by Mr G.A. Jeffries. The exhibition comprised views of the most important public buildings and places in London, the British Isles, India, Australia, &c., and several of the finest cathedrals in England.'

The Arboretum Lodge opening on to Rosehill Street, looking on to the site of the former 'Crystal Palace', built by subscription in 1845 on an extension of the original park and no longer there after World War One. (Photo: Andrew Butterton)

There were outings too, like that enjoyed by 100 workhouse children to the Arboretum in August 1878, conveyed in horse-drawn carriages. They got 'an excellent tea with plumcake and ginger-bread' in the 'Crystal Palace' there, 'after which the boys were presented by Mrs Currey with knives, tops, whips, and kites; and the girls with books and battledores and shuttlecocks'. In January 1888 the Union inmates all went to the almost-new Grand Theatre for a special performance of *Dick Whittington and his Cat* and in July 1900 inmates who were mentally ill were taken in a four-horse carriage out to Tutbury Castle, where they were served with tobacco and given donkey rides, to finish with 'a substantial cake tea'. Overall, the impression of *Mercury* reports is of regulated charity with a decidedly human face.

Health hazard

The housing problem we have already noted and which was never properly tackled in Victorian times in Derby obviously had consequences for health. This was particularly so in the earlier part of the period before the national Board of Health report in 1849 that led to improvements in drainage and sewage disposal during the decades that followed. A hint of the after-effects of previous defects comes in one of the innumerable advertisements for quack medicines, this one for 'DAFFY'S ELIXIR' in July 1837, that featured in the *Mercury*. This example referred to 'those distressing Bowel Complaints which so often occur in this Variable climate, frequently attended with severe spasms, or cramp, in the chest or stomach; ... which prevailed so much during the last Summer and Autumn as to acquire the denomination of English Cholera.' More precise evidence came in the Registrar General's Report in November 1846: '[Parish] of St Peter – Deaths 172. This return is above the average. The prevailing epidemic is bowel complaint, of which 31 fatal cases have occurred. There have also been 6 fatal cases of typhus. St Alkmund –The number of deaths registered this quarter is 109, which is 35 above the average, diarrhoea having been very prevalent.'

We might read into the figures for admission to the Derby (Provident) Dispensary on Bridge Gate confirmation of the bad effect of poor drainage on the health of poorer Derbeians. According to the *Mercury* in May 1846 the Dispensary, on the other side of town from the imposing Derbyshire General Infirmary and therefore close to the older textile mills and foundries, had been set up specifically 'to secure medical aid for all those amongst the working classes who are too poor to procure it for themselves'. If families had been in receipt of help from the Poor Law Guardians they had free treatment. Otherwise if a Dispensary 'member' were over 14 years of age he/she paid a penny a week, under that age the fee was a half-penny. However, Dispensary figures published in the *Mercury* show that there was some increase in illness during the summer and autumn months, which could well have been due to poor drainage and water supply. During that same month, at a Town Council meeting in which the Mayor expressed regret at the death statistics in Derby, Councillor Dr Brent stated that they

The Derbyshire Royal Infirmary (DRI) in a photo of about 1904. The 'Royal' was added to the name in 1891 after the Queen laid the foundation stone for a major extension (nearest the camera) done in red-brick Jacobean pavilion style. (Courtesy: Derby Local Studies Library)

proved that the town was more unhealthy than 15 other manufacturing centres. The implication was that Alderman Douglas Fox, the Medical Officer of Health, was too complacent in his attitude.

Indeed, Alderman Fox had to concede in November that year at another meeting at the Guildhall that many owners of property did not fulfil their obligation to keep the drainage channels clear. How far should they be forced to do so? The Alderman admitted that 'the noxious smells which at present escaped from the untrapped gullies affected most seriously the well-being of the population; for it was past dispute, that a great deal of disease arose from this cause. There were 1050 gully holes in Derby at that moment, 59 or 60 only of which were tapped, or only 1 in 17.' There was also the case of the Markeaton Brook: 'all kinds of filth and impurities were cast into it. It was a depository for filth and dead cats and dogs, which were thrown into it, and left to putrify all the summer.' Dr Brent declared 'he had in one day counted four dead dogs which lay on the surface of the brook-course'. Also during November (1846), the *Chesterfield and Derby Reporter* recorded at least 16 cases of fever in the previous four weeks in a single terrace off the Ashbourne Road. The waste from this particular terrace emptied into 'a large open ditch at the foot of Mr Richardson's grounds' where it lay three or four inches deep for some time and left a filthy putrid deposit.' The editor of the *Mercury* called for an addition to the Borough rate, declaring that 'public health is of far higher value than so many pounds, shillings, and pence'.

The Council simply had to respond to the government's national inquiry into public health and appoint a new Borough Board of Health to take things forward. This set about the drainage and sewage problem and as a result by 1856 the *Mercury* was able to report that Derby's mortality rate had gone down from 27.75 to 21.75 per 1,000 persons. But there was a remaining problem. In September 1867, when the Poor Law Guardians discussed the health of the town, their deliberations were focussed on a letter from the Mayor drawing attention to the frequency (82, no less, in one area) of cases of diarrhoea in the workhouse district, together with 'the filthy condition of some of the houses in the parishes of the town inhabited by the lower classes'.

Final reckoning

The 1870s were the last decade when Derby Dispensary records were published. For example, in October 1878 there were a record 6,307 people on the books. That autumn saw the highest number of weekly sick enrolments (37), next being the summer (28). So little had changed on that particular front. In 1883 the Hospital for Sick Children was opened on North Street, just a block or two away from the Dispensary. The Hospital must have at least partially taken the place of the Dispensary. Its statistics for in-patients during the first 20 years of its existence changed in exactly the opposite way to those of its out-patients department. Whereas the average monthly admissions halved between 1888 and 1900 (26 down to 13), those for out-patients nearly doubled (from 67 to 118 – there were 128 in 1897). The average number on the books more than doubled in that time, from 83 to 173 (with a maximum of 208 in July 1900). But could it be that many parents could not afford to support their children inside the hospital in those far-off pre-National Health days?

One thing was crystal clear by 1900: far more people were being born in Derby homes each year than were dying of whatever cause and the population was climbing steeply. In fact it went from 81,000 in 1881 to 94,000 in 1891 to over 100,000 in 1901. Whether it was due to the improvements in the sewage and sanitary arrangements, together with an entirely new clean water supply, combined with the town's modest size in a setting of surpassingly beautiful countryside, Derby had the lowest monthly death-rate in a series of selected large towns in 1897: 16.6, compared with London's 17.6, Leicester's 17.9, Nottingham's 19.2, Birmingham's 21.9 and Wolverhampton's 24.5, all per 1,000 persons. However, August was still the most deadly month for all six of those towns in 1897. Was it still a case of persistently defective hygiene and drainage in warm weather? There could be sudden epidemics as well, as in the second week of January 1900, which returned the highest weekly death-rate for the year (69). Alas, the final health statistics in Victorian times reveal another shadow over the homes of Derby folk. While an edition of the *Mercury* in October 1900 hailed the resolution of the Town Council to appoint a female sanitary inspector, as in so many spheres only following in the wake of other towns, the Medical Officer Dr Laurie, in his reported welcome for the proposal, spoke of 'the heavy death-rate of young children in Derby'. From the previous August the paper had published weekly statistics of infant mortality. If we take an average of 18 sets of figures given by the end of that year, we might conclude that there were 193 infant deaths for every 1,000 live births in Derby, or a near 20 percent death-rate for young children! In the week ending 10 October the figure rose to 296, nearly 30 percent! This is surely a shocking statistic. How can we possibly imagine the immensity of grief it coldly represents for the Derby families of the time, probably concentrated in those grim left-over courts and grimy terraces. Progress was indeed slow and costly.

And Derby was not alone. The abyss between rich and poor, which of course was there in Georgian times, became more visible in the Victorian age because factory employment concentrated the populace in manufacturing towns and cities like Derby. The result was the national problem uncovered by the outbreak of the Boer War in 1898. Four out of 10 young men volunteering for the British army had to be turned down because their physique would not have stood the strain. They suffered rotten teeth, weak hearts, poor eyesight and hearing, and weren't tall enough. For the second time in 20 years infantry regiments had to reduce their minimum height requirement to five feet, six inches less than in 1880! When an inquiry was set up to investigate, it reported in 1904 (three years into the reign of King Edward VII) that Board School boys of 10 to 12 years of age were on average five inches shorter than those at private schools. This meant that if an inspector had been allowed to wander from the Ashbourne Road School to Derby School and then out to Repton he would probably have encountered a range of height among respective pupils of the same age conforming to that statistic. It was not surprising at all. Factory inspectors found that working girls suffered from the same deficiencies: short, poorly developed, sallow cheeks, bad teeth. They were of course the mothers. Breast-feeding had declined because of the demands of factory employment and many mothers were unable to produce milk. Babies might be given the cheapest food, such as sweetened condensed milk, breeder of rickets. The poorest relied on a mixture of flour and water, milk-like only to look at. It would be a vital task of the Edwardians to try to change this for the better.

CHAPTER 5

Places of Learning and Prayer

DERBY TOWN AND COUNTY MUSEUM – Sir Francis Darwin, of Sydnope, has made a handsome present to this institution, of which the following are a part: a racoon and an opossum from South America – an Indian bow from North America, an ancient crossbow, of very curious device – a bear's skull, and a New Zealand warclub, and a head and antlers of the Irish elk, very perfect. This huge type of the Cervus genus is now an extinct race in that island.

(*Derby Mercury*, 8 February 1837)

Queen Victoria's uncle William was still king when the editor of the *Mercury* began a campaign to establish a museum for the people of Derby, underlining the cause with the flourish: 'The Duke of Devonshire has graciously promised to lay the foundation stone of the intended building'. The original impulse was to form a geological collection which could be useful to a prospecting miner. But only three weeks later the paper announced the Darwin family gift, which obviously had a world-wide geographical reference. There was an urgent need for somewhere suitable for displaying the multiplying objects: in July the same year 'E.S. Chandos-Pole, Esq.' handed over 'a Stuffed Kangaroo of the musk kind, a Stuffed Mexican Deer; the Head of a four-horned Chilean Ram; also a remarkably fine male Lama, which is now undergoing the process of stuffing, and will make a valuable Zoological specimen'. Other bequests reported in 1846 included 'An Egyptian Mummy, of great antiquity and value, and three large Original Paintings presented by the Executors of the late Joseph Strutt, Esq.'

While it took over 40 years for a proper museum building to arrive through the generosity of the town's leading Member of Parliament in Victorian times, Thomas Bass, a temporary home was found for the strange educational objects in the Athenaeum Club building on Victoria Street (called Brookside when construction started on it), completed in 1839. The

The Free Library of 1879, gift of Thomas Bass, the town's premier Liberal MP and benefactor, to Victorian Derby. (Photo: Andrew Butterton)

PVBLIC·LIBRARY

·AND·MVS

arrangement was obviously a success, as a report presented to the town's Natural History Society in November 1846 makes clear. It mentions many visitors ('Strangers') who expressed their gratitude for the facility, also school parties 'accompanied by their Tutors'.

Ownership

The growing collection was obviously the responsibility of the Natural History Society. When they offered it to the Town Council in January 1856 as possibly 'an institution of great value to the inhabitants of Derby, highly creditable to the town, and well adapted to meet the wants of its rapidly expanding population', the Councillors turned it down by 12 votes to nine! This despite a letter to the *Mercury* the previous week from 'A FRIEND OF THE WORKING CLASSES' urging Derby to follow the example of the 'admirable Salford Borough Royal Museum and Library, situated in Peel Park, Manchester', opened just six years earlier. It would be, according to the writer, 'an inestimable boon' to the 'working classes of this town and neighbourhood'. It was not to be.

In 1879 the town at last caught up with the likes of Salford, at nil cost to the Council of course, with Thomas Bass paying for a combined Free Public Library and Museum, to which would soon be added an Art Gallery. The building would include another of Bass's pet projects, the reconstruction of the panelled room from demolished Exeter House by the river where Bonnie Prince Charlie decided on his fateful retreat to Scotland in 1745.

There were further bequests to the rehoused collection; for example in March 1888 two 'fine otters', the male 'taken in the Trent near Drakelow', and both 'prepared and mounted by Mr A.S. Hutchinson, of London Road, taxidermist to the Museum'. However, that October, 'A DERBYSHIRE RESIDENT' complained to the *Mercury* that 'the collection of Derbyshire treasures is very incomplete'. The Museum obviously lacked 'a case specially devoted to fossils and specimens from Derbyshire coal mines, and another of the various products found in Derbyshire lead mines, and likewise other Derbyshire geologic and mineral specimens by themselves'. So there was a way to go yet, despite its collection of remains from Cresswell Crags, a specific focus of attention for this particular visitor.

Nevertheless, the new Museum and Art Gallery did attract many other visitors. According to a *Mercury* report in January 1888, 2,952 people entered the Museum portals during the two days of the previous Christmas holidays (including Boxing Day) and 1,445 the Art Gallery, 'a number which compares very favourably with those visiting similar institutions in other towns'.

Ragged-trousered scholarship

It surely must be doubtful whether the Museum and Art Gallery admissions will have included any of the scholars from Back Parker Street. This was at one time the location of the Derby Ragged School, where from 1849 an effort was made to impart knowledge to the children of the destitute. Home to many of these might well have been nearby Willow Row or Walker Lane. The school room depended for its maintenance on public generosity. According to an article in the *Mercury* in January 1856, it was 'full to overflowing' with about 90 pupils and was 'more highly prized than ever' by their families. The school's objective was 'to instruct the ignorant, to re-claim the vicious, to elevate the degraded' – strongly moral

Victorian stuff. Indeed, the Mayor that year when chairing the annual control meeting spoke of ragged schools providing an 'important check' to juvenile crime. On the one hand, the children were given a Christmas-day treat of 'hot sausage, rolls, and plum pudding' followed by a presentation of 'smocks and smock-frocks'. On the other, they were put through an annual examination in 'Holy Scripture, … arithmetic, geography, &c.', and had specimens of their writing and needlework displayed to the interested parties. There is evidence from a *Mercury* report of one of these occasions that pupils could be street-wise as well as school-wise. In the course of the examining interviews conducted in front of an audience it became apparent that many children associated the geographical areas known as Ireland and Scotland with types of whiskey, one 'young urchin' distinguishing the two products by describing them in turn as 'a drop of the cratur' and 'Mountain Dew' – to the amusement of the patrons. A large number of prizes were given, including 'work boxes, cases, books, and useful things'.

The editor of the *Mercury* roasted his readership in August that year over the fact that 'the meagre sum of £286 a year' which the Ragged School cost to run was hard to come by. Its activities needed extending both backwards and forwards. On the one hand, children had to be six years old to be admitted, leaving out the 'many ragged and destitute children between the ages of two and six, who might share in the benefits of the school'; on the other, a night-school for older pupils was an urgent priority. The annual school report provides us with a glimpse of the life experience of these children in 1856. The places of the 68 pupils who had left during the year (out of the 86 on the books) had been filled immediately. No wonder. Most got a daily meal 'at a time when much suffering has been experienced from the scarce quantity of work and the high price of provisions'. Over a quarter of children left for other schools 'having improved in their circumstances' (father had got a job?). Nearly the same number left for work and a handful for the workhouse, presumably because their family background had deteriorated. The need for Ragged Schools, the original building for one of which still stands in Chesterfield, would remain for another 30 years until Gladstone's Liberal Government at last took the matter of the elementary education of the nation's children seriously in the 1870s.

Towards Board School

Families who could afford it would either employ a governess or tutor at home or send their offspring to a private school. The *Mercury* carried many advertisements for the latter. The Misses Lallemand were running a school in Bridge Gate in January 1837 and William Y. Wilson ran one in Agard Street. In January 1846 Mrs Timmins was presiding over a 'Preparatory School for Young Gentlemen' in Full Street and that February Mrs Beeland was promoting her school at Spondon House. In January 1856 the Misses Sowter reminded pupils of their reopening date at 7 North Parade. By 1892 parents who could afford it had the Derby High School for Girls with 145 places on the Osmaston Road. By January 1901 it was also advertising a 'Kindergarten' for boys as well as girls and the 'HEAD MISTRESS, Miss C.A.TUKE' would be 'at the High School to receive Parents after 13 January'. There was a branch in Friar Gate and boarders could stay in Hartington Street with Mrs Godfrey and Miss A. Godfrey and would have the benefit of 'Gymnasium, Playground, Scholarships'.

Before 1870 most children would attend primary schools run by two societies which rivalled each other along separate religious lines. National Schools, like the one on Curzon

The Ashbourne Road Board Schools of 1879, most important surviving relic with the Becket Street offices of Liberal Prime Minister Gladstone's Education reforms. (Photo: Andrew Butterton)

Street, were clearly supported by the *Mercury* 'for the education of the Poor in the principles of the established Church'. Lancastrian Schools, like the one on Orchard Street (President, 'His Grace, the Duke of Devonshire', Chair, Joseph Strutt, Esq.) welcomed Non-conformists. So in May 1837 Orchard Street recorded an average attendance of 230 pupils out of a total of 290, all 'required to attend on the public worship of Almighty God' with 100 going to 'the Established Church' (C of E) and 190 'with other classes of Christians'. In March 1846, 216 pupils were examined at Curzon Street. 'They appeared to be familiar not only with the leading events, but also with the minutiae of Scripture history, and with but few exceptions, to comprehend the substance of the church catechism, the words of which they could all fluently repeat.'

Attendance at these schools was voluntary. From the 1870s Derby parents like those in every other town in the country were obliged to send their children free of charge to elementary schools organised locally under the authority of 'School Boards'. The Derby School Board Office was located in Becket Street. Parents who were members of the various types of Christian churches had their desire for their children to have appropriate religious instruction respected. And so there were also Roman Catholic and Wesleyan (Methodist) schools in addition to the newly constructed and specifically styled 'Board' Schools. If we look at the records of attendance published in the *Mercury* from time to time, though not consistently, we find that between 1878 and 1900 there was an increase of 64 percent in registered pupils and an average increase in attendance levels of 9 percent. By 1900 Board Schools were winning out in any competition in places taken between the various types of school. Average attendance at them increased from 19 percent to 51 percent of the total elementary pupil population while Church of England schools decreased from 60 percent to 42 percent, Roman Catholic from 5 percent to 2.5 percent and Wesleyan from 12 percent to 4.5 percent.

Many teachers, if not parents, were very critical of what went on in the classrooms. They voiced their concerns at meetings of the South Derbyshire Teachers' Association. They were paid by results, according to how many pupils Government inspectors considered up to standard in annual tests. The business of tests was an explosive issue well over a century ago! Teachers felt compelled to drill all their pupils to the particular demands of the test. In May 1888 the *Mercury* reported the Association's President, the Head of Milford School, giving his verdict on the system: 'it reduces the strong child and the weakly, the well fed and the ill fed, the intelligent and the dull, to one dead level of uniformity; the teacher is turned into a great grinder, the child into a mere grant-earning machine'. It 'handicaps the smart ones, and it is evil to the dull. It is, indeed, the dull children who require the most encouragement...' At another Association meeting that December the Head of Crich School declared that 'intelligent teaching is discouraged and 'cramming' for 'passes' takes its place'.

For the older pupil

Well-off young Derbeians might be sent out to Repton beside the sylvan Trent. There was no system of secondary education for most ordinary adolescents until 1902, by which time the Government realised how far behind our Continental neighbours England was sliding in the matter of education. Parents who could afford a moderate day-boy fee might well have been interested in the *Mercury* advertisement in January 1856 for the 'GRAMMAR' School, detailing its hopefully eager and waiting academic staff: 'JOHN HUDSON, Head-Master. ASSISTANT MASTERS, the Revd G.T.HUTCHINSON. Mr W.T.BARBER, B.A.' Seven years later Derby School, which was being promoted here, moved from Friar Gate to noble St Helen's House. In the 1860s it had a progressive and energetic Head, the Revd Walter Clark MA, who wanted the school to compete with Nottingham Grammar in the matter of access for Derby boys to the prestigious Oxford and Cambridge universities. He offered to give an 'Exhibition' (place) worth £60 a year out of his own pocket if 'two other gentlemen be willing to found two other Exhibitions of the same value'. This move had the strong support of the *Mercury* editor (December 1867). The Revd Clark, who presided over a visit to the School by the Prince of Wales (later King Edward VII) in 1872 and in memory of that royal occasion had a large additional block rather uncomfortably added to St Helen's House on its north side, was still there to persuade the prince to ennoble the extra building with a repeat visit in 1881.

The Victorian additions to Derby School (formerly St Helen's House), with the headteacher's house in the far corner between the teaching block, including the hall and laboratories opened by the Prince of Wales in 1881 on the right, and the Chapel, added a few years later, on the left. (Photo: Andrew Butterton)

The model for Derby School in Victorian times was the 'Public School', the nearest example being Repton. The connection with the Established Church was 'cemented' by another addition in the shape of a Gothic-style red-brick chapel in the 1880s on the north side of the school yard and that with the Armed Services by the inclusion of a Cadet Corps. The Corps' annual inspection at the Drill Hall in Newland Street was reported in the *Mercury* in July 1897 when regimental Commander Colonel Sparkes was 'perfectly satisfied' with their drill 'from beginning to end'. On the manner in which the boys fired their guns, 'he had no fault to find except that in one or two instances some of the boys had their fingers on the

The Diocesan Training College of 1850. The architect was Henry Isaac Stephens in red-brick 'Tudoresque' mode. He included a distinctive calling card above the main entrance. (Photos: Andrew Butterton)

triggers when they should not have had them there'. Quite so! When the inspection was over 'the boys were marched back to school'.

All this was of course to do with the education of the male of the Derby species. But, in addition to the Derby College of Art opened on Green Lane in 1878 in a handsome stone concoction of pepper-pot towers and pointy gables to rival the Free Library, almost but not quite completed then in the middle of town below, from back in 1850 bright Derby girls had the opportunity of training to be teachers in their native town. Some might see the siting of the Derby Lonsdale Diocesan Training College on Uttoxeter New Road as a very appropriate counter-balancing act. It was put up, designed by Derby architect Henry Isaac Stephens, almost directly opposite the eight-year-old resting place of deceased local worthies. Was it a case of youthful hope soothing a final reckoning? At any rate, over Stephens's ornate entrance is the legend 'For Training Schoolmistresses'. By the end of the century the students here were perhaps matching the accomplishments of their counterparts in Green Lane in a sister art. If the artists had the tradition of the town's greatest son, painter Joseph Wright, behind them, in May 1900 their New Road sisters won the enthusiastic approval of composer Sir John Stainer. His most famous work, the cantata *The Crucifixion*, may be familiar to many older fans of choral music, though his fame would soon be eclipsed by the younger genius Edward Elgar. But his business in coming to Derby was to inspect the standard in music at the Diocesan College. At the end of the concert put on for his benefit, according to the *Mercury* reporter, he made a few remarks 'expressing his pleasure at finding that the college still retained its high standard of musical excellence, and thanking the students and all concerned for the part they had played in preparing for his delectation so enjoyable a programme'.

After school

Those who missed out on 'adequate' schooling in Derby had one channel for trying to catch up in some way. In October 1837 the *Mercury* reported on the opening of a splendid new hall

PLACES OF LEARNING AND PRAYER

at the Mechanics' Institution, which had started life in the Wardwick in 1825 and possessed 'a well-furnished and commodious Reading Room supplied with all the leading Periodicals, as well as accommodation for Classes in Drawing, Chemistry, and Music; and two evenings a week a Class for instruction in the French language, and a School for Reading, Writing, and Arithmetic'. It was open every day except Sundays from 10am to 10pm and every other Wednesday held discussions on literature and science. The new hall was 'beautifully decorated' and 'excellently lighted up with gas'.

It was the venue for a series of 'Popular Lectures' like the one advertised in October 1837 for the price of a small subscription: 'On the Physical, Intellectual, and Moral Constitution of Man'. Later that year there was another series on the 'Instinct of Animals' by the town's Medical Officer, Dr Douglas Fox. In February 1878 the *Mercury* announced a series of just two Cookery Lectures, with practical demonstrations, given by the Head of the Liverpool School of Cookery. In January 1888 the theatre of learning moved to the Guildhall for a series of 12 lectures on 'Sound and Music' by a Cambridge lecturer sponsored by a new 'Derby University Extension Society'. This, according to the *Mercury,* had as its object 'the providing of the means of higher education for persons of all classes and of both sexes engaged in the ordinary occupations of life by means of University teachers for those unable to go to the University'.

For the general Derby public there were from time to time one-off celebrity lectures, like the one reported on by the *Mercury* in September 1846 at the Athenaeum room by the Revd J. Crabb from Southampton on the subject of 'THE ENGLISH GYPSIES'. The speaker deplored on the one hand the often shabby treatment gypsies received from so-called Christians and on the other his subjects' frequent dependence on fortune-telling. At the same venue in September 1856 a couple of lectures aimed directly, even offensively, at a far more significant minority of the population were delivered in 'the sombre garb of a monk, wearing on his robes a large black cloak' by one Alessandro Gavazzi. It was a second visit to Derby by this 'striking and impressive man', a sort of exotic Ian Paisley, who was able this time to deliver in English his no-holds-barred attack on the Roman Catholic Church, peeling away what he claimed was its mask to reveal 'the ugly face of Rome'. In far more temperate mode in November/December the same year, back at the Mechanics' Hall, 'George Grossmith, Esq., of London' gave two lectures on books by the literary man of the moment Charles Dickens.

Far more in the celebrity class were the offerings later in the century. In May 1878 the Co-operative Hall in Albert Street was packed to the rafters, with 'hundreds turned away', to hear Mrs Annie Besant, notorious for her advocacy of socialism, non-belief and, far worse, birth-control, for which she had had her children ordered to be taken from her the previous year! Her subject that evening was 'Poverty and Social Vice' and she had been accepted by the Co-op Management after the Temperance and Drill Halls, with far more seating, had refused to host her. In the same edition as its report on the proceedings the *Mercury* also published a letter signed 'A WORKING MAN' protesting at the Co-op's decision to 'be the means of introducing to our town a teacher who unreservedly avows her atheism' and with whom, quoting the Master of the Rolls, 'no chaste woman would associate'. The *Mercury* reporter pointedly described Mrs Besant as having 'primly coiffed luxuriant black hair, matching dark and expressive eyes', with an unusually 'ornate' costume. Obviously *une femme fatale*! She was accompanied by her young daughter in order not to have her taken away. The reporter thought her lecture 'not worth listening to by a cultivated person, and feminine logic everywhere protruded itself'. When she had finished 'it took over four or five police officers to enable Mrs Besant to reach the cab; as it departed the crowd hooted and cheered'.

Much less controversial would have been the October lecture at the Drill Hall by 'MR.STANLEY, the African explorer', his subject 'Through the Dark Continent'. After stating that he had lost 150 men on his expedition, he 'described the effect of seeing white people again after "nothing but the bronze and ebony skins of the aborigines" [obviously a general patronising if not offensive term at that time]' and added that 'he had never addressed a more sympathetic audience'! And in October 1897 at the Albert Hall (Mechanics' Institute), headlined 'A GREAT MOUNTAINEER IN DERBY', Edward Whymper lectured on climbing in the Alps and Andes, including a 'very vivid description of his own great achievement – the conquest of the "peerless and incomparable" Matterhorn'.

Cultural peep-shows

Derbeians could enjoy from time to time various temporary displays and exhibitions to complement the permanent collection of objects which, as we have seen, were in the charge of first the Derby Natural History Society and later the town's Museum and Art Gallery. In June 1837 the *Mercury* recommended to its readership a show of 'Egyptian Antiquities' at 'Mr Moseley's Marble Museum, Corn Market'. In September 1838 'The Whale Exhibition' arrived on the Brookside (soon to be renamed Victoria Street). It was described as 'the skeleton of a whale of immense dimensions, probably the largest that ever came under human observation; and which has been shown to admiring crowds in most of the towns of the kingdom'. In January 1878 for 11 nights at the Drill Hall 'every evening at 8' was exhibited 'the largest and most costly Diorama in the World, illustrating the whole of the British possessions abroad, and the principal incidents in the War in the East [between Russia and Turkey], realising in a marvellous and realistic manner the dread realities of the Campaign'.

The Sabbath

As the 'warmly applauded' Gavazzi's performances and Mrs Besant's reception tell us, religious belief was a decidedly serious matter in Victorian Derby. The town was a hot centre of the Sabbatarian craze, the struggle to keep Sunday holy in the 1830s and 1840s. While the Church of England strove through new church building (as in Holy Trinity, Christ Church, St Paul's, St Luke's, St Anne's, St Barnabas's, St Thomas's, St Andrew's and St Chad's) to reach out to the industrial workers around the edges of the old central heart of town in competition with the Methodists, Congregationalists and Roman Catholics, Established Church attendance would have been largely a middle-class habit as elsewhere in England, though working-class children crowded the Sunday Schools. The campaign to keep Sunday holy could be regarded as an attempt at social control, to put some restraint on the freedom to do what they wanted on the ever-increasing ranks of labourers skilled and unskilled. On the other hand, as in the case of the 'tramway servants' later on in the century, it might help to ensure at least one complete day of rest in the week. This was certainly the hard edge of the case for 'Lord's Day Observance' made at a meeting at the Bell Inn, Sadler Gate, in March

St Paul's, Chester Green, in Victorian Gothic style, in a print made probably in 1850, the year of its consecration. It was later added to at the expense of local foundry boss Alfred Haslam and is an example of the Church of England's outreach programme to serve expanding 'suburban' communities. (Courtesy: Derby Local Studies Library)

1837. The following May a Petition to Parliament displayed for signature at 'Mr Bemrose's, in the Market Place' campaigned against the running of the Royal Mail on Sunday, thus depriving 'Guards, Coachmen, Horsekeepers, Postmasters, Clerks, Letter-carriers, Postmen, &c.' of their Sabbath rest and privileges'.

However, the objective could be much broader. In August 1846 the *Mercury* published a letter from Joseph Padfield, Spondon, attacking the bathing in the Derwent that went on on Sundays, and the parents who allowed their children to do this rather than sending them to Sunday School. The drownings that occurred were, according to the writer, far from accidental. A 'jealous God' punishes 'the desecrators of his Sabbath'. The *Mercury* itself was far from unsympathetic! In February 1856 the editor declared himself against the opening of museums and showplaces like the Crystal Palace in London on Sunday. Making free with Sunday was what they did on the Continent, associated with Roman Catholicism. The pages of the *Mercury* were hot with anti-Catholic feeling. Sabbatarianism was definitely a Protestant affair. And yet, as the years went by, the prejudice must have softened. A notably sympathetic

The Unitarian Chapel on Friar Gate where Joseph Strutt worshipped and where his funeral took place in 1843, just three years after his gift of the Arboretum to the town. The original building dated from the end of the 17th century and Strutt would not have known the porches or the plane trees added after 1860. (Courtesy: Derby Local Studies Library)

tone can surely be felt in the *Mercury* report in May 1856 of the return to Derby of the 'reverend mother' of the Convent and 15 of her nuns from the war in the Crimea. They had 'attended the sick at Scutari and the Crimea during the whole of the War'. These ladies 'were received by the Revd T. Sing and the Revd J. Daniels, who had a carriage drawn by four greys, with postilions, waiting at the station to receive them. The whole party drove through the town to the convent at about four o'clock in the afternoon.'

For worship and prayer

Derby's Roman Catholics were the first religious group to make a mark on the town's skyline in the reign of Queen Victoria. She had been in Buckingham Palace just a year when the foundation stone of St Mary's was put down. When finished in 1839 the entrance would be 13 steps up from the pavements of Bridge Gate. Architect Pugin's noble Gothic-style tower was to be topped with a spire that was never built. Our present-day view of St Mary's from the top of Iron Gate was destined to be blotted out for well over a century seven years later by the Derby Church of England's response to the Catholic challenge – the repeat-Gothic tower and spire of St Alkmund's, designed by native architect Henry Isaac Stephens. It replaced an old, genuinely mediaeval, predecessor on the site. It must have pleased the *Mercury*'s editor no end. His comment on the foundation of St Mary's was: 'We say, that no man can shut his eyes to the fact, that the Roman Catholic party are now industriously bent, and are applying every energy, to get back the dominion they once had'. The cowled Gavazzi himself could not have put it plainer!

Stephens went on to design the Diocesan Teacher Training College on Uttoxeter New Road just four years later and then a church for Alvaston opened in 1856. As we saw earlier when proving conclusively that Derby is above all a Victorian town, many more bell-towers and steeples would signal to a distant observer the presence of numerous chapels and churches added to religious assets during the century. Some of these towers, like the strikingly designed one at St Luke's off Stockbrook Street, were sited to serve rapidly expanding suburbs short on service of any kind. And not quickly enough for the editor of the *Mercury,* who in February 1878 complained of the lack of any kind of church in the 30 acres of new housing between the Burton Road and Normanton, 'where not a single house stood a few months ago'. The people there, he moaned, 'cannot without the greatest inconvenience, attend the places of worship in either town or country, the distance in either case providing an all but insuperable barrier'.

From the *Mercury*, too, we get an occasional glimpse of what was happening Sunday by Sunday inside these buildings dedicated to worship and prayer. For example, in January 1856 it printed a letter from an All Saints' parishioner complaining of the amount of coughing that went on in the town's most senior religious structure. He or she wailed that regardless of age or sex people with 'deranged breathing and sneezing organs' insisted on going to church and so 'very shortly either in solo, glee or chorus disturb the meditation of the whole congregation by their variable, tuneless, electrical irrepressible catarrhal appeals'. The minister had to endure a barrage of 'unseemly ejaculatory nasal and vocal interruptions'. On one recent Sunday, at a service taken by the Revd Phillip Gell, 'a more discordant and simultaneous crowing was seldom heard at a poultry show'.

To end our service inspection on a more suitable serious note, in May 1856 the *Mercury* provided the reader with the texts from the Bible on which the ministers in the various

Interior of St Luke's, Parliament Street. Completed in 1870, again in Gothic style, it was designed by architects Stephens and Frederick Robinson. It served an expanding area of terraced housing around the far end of Stockbrook Street. This image dates from 1914. (Courtesy: Derby Local Studies Library)

Exterior of St Luke's, *c.*1870. (Courtesy: Derby Local Studies Library)

churches in the town based their sermons on the Sunday set aside by the Government to give thanks for the end of the Crimean War. Here are a few samples: 'Is it not good if peace and truth be in my day?'(*Kings*); 'Shout, for the Lord hath given you the city' (*Joshua*); 'As the nations which the Lord destroyeth before your very face, so shall ye perish' (*Deuteronomy*); 'nation shall not lift up sword against nation, neither shall they learn war any more' (*Isaiah*); 'He maketh peace in thy borders' (*Psalms*); 'Then believed they his words; they sang His praise; they soon forgot His works' (*Psalms*). Of course we don't have a record of the commentary the clergymen made on the basis of these texts, but most of them would seem to be leading away from the expression of a triumphalist attitude to the sad event that had come to its end. The Derby Victorians were surely a seriously sober bunch for the most part, their feet firmly on Derbyshire ground, though their ultimate hope might be elsewhere.

CHAPTER 6

Workplaces

FATAL ACCIDENT. – On Thursday last a child, named Jane Bamford, was accidentally killed at the mill occupied by Mr Lawton, in Wright Street, in this town, in consequence of her clothes becoming entangled in the machinery. An inquest was held on the following day before Mr B.T. Balguy, coroner, and a verdict of 'accidental death' returned.'

(*Derby Mercury*, October 1838)

The presence of children among potentially lethal machinery mercifully decreased through Victoria's long reign, in Derby as elsewhere. Their earnings were essential to working-class

Looking towards the centre of town from the site of the Britannia Foundry, Derby's premier ironworks, source of the GNR railway bridges over the Derwent and Friar Gate. (Photo: Andrew Butterton)

families given the comparatively poor wages their parents were able to obtain unless their skills were special and in the shortest supply.

Derby's prosperity depended upon working mills of various kinds, silk, cotton, iron, flour and so on, apart from the gigantic Midland Railway complex, and also upon a host of smaller workshops. Most views of the town painted or photographed from any sort of distance in the 19th century are punctuated by the thin stalks of works chimneys, with or without an accompanying wisp of smoke. We have already referred to paintings in the Goodey collection held by the museum. One of these, titled 'Derby from the east, 1857', by H.L. Pratt, includes a fair sprinkling of stacks clustering around the familiar church towers and steeples. A more powerful image was provided by Raymond Dearn in his later view from the Great Northern Railway Bridge between Haslam's Union Mills on the Derwent left bank and the Britannia Mills on the right. A clutch of chimneys on either side of the river spout a collective smoke haze from which the tower of All Saints' only just manages to stay aloof in the background. More concentrated still, though more lightly and pleasingly washed in a watercolour medium, is A.J. Keene's 1894 image of the Sharon Chemical Company's works. The Little Eaton branch of the Derby Canal fronts a continuous wall of workshop roofs with a score of stacks gushing steam and smoke to form a billowing low cloud that this time leaves a gap for old All Saints' looming behind. But perhaps the two most extreme images of our productive town in the Victorian era are C.T. Moore's *The Morledge in Fairtime, 1882* and A.J. Keene's *Work-a-day Derby* of 1905 (admittedly four years into the following century, but still essentially a Victorian scene). In the one fairground merry-making is backed by a host of smoking chimney stacks, some belonging to nearby houses but most to factories jostling the domes, towers and steeples that support the grim hulk of the Shot Tower. In the other we are able to look down from North Parade towards invisible Derwentside lost among long ranks of workshop and foundry roofs; steam bursts lighten a pall of dark smoke supported on the black pillars of mill chimneys.

It is not a pretty sight, but surely hugely atmospheric and mightily impressive.

Glimpses over the wall

Sale notices, details of accidents, reports of strikes, the fortunately only occasional disaster, and the content of bosses' speeches provided the reader of the *Mercury* with fleeting opportunities to peer inside the mill by proxy and gain some hints as to what was going on there. For example, in December 1837 the Markeaton Mill was open to offers from 'Colour Manufacturers, Cement Manufacturers, Rail Road Contractors, &c.' It was described as a water mill, and was said to be 'four stories [sic] high, with an upright shaft from the water wheel throughout, capable of having any kind of machinery attached to it'. It also had a 'steam boiler, large bleaching becks, vats, stoves, and apparatus, for the manufacture of Sulphate of Byrites or Dutch Lead, Colours, and Roman Cement on a large scale'. In April 1846, on the death of its boss Thomas Wright, one of the most prestigious of the town's firms was up for sale, namely the Britannia Iron Foundry 'situated near St Mary's-Bridge, in the Borough of Derby'. It was described as 'an old established and thriving firm' and was 'now in full work' behind 'a spacious frontage, with convenient wharfs, to the River Derwent'. A would-be purchaser would find 'large moulding shops, smith's and joiner's shops, turning shops, sheds, engine-room, offices, ware-rooms, stabling, manager's house &c. &c.'

The River Derwent from Exeter Bridge looking north towards the Old Silk Mill. The photo was taken by Keene in June 1891 after the southernmost section of the mill (formerly the Doubling Shop) had been demolished. Other enterprises line the river banks. (Courtesy: Derby Museum and Art Gallery)

In February 1855, in addition to the historic Old Silk Mill now over 130 years old, to be leased from the Corporation having 'lately undergone very substantial and extensive repairs', there was far more detail about the Park Foundry in Liversage Street, also up for leasing. Whoever wanted it badly enough would get:

> ... 20 horse high pressure steam engine, with boiler, nearly new; one 6-horse horizontal double cylinder steam engine; valuable self-acting planing machine, with double heads; screwing machine, cool shafting dust mill, large cupola, large and very powerful foundry crane, five iron foundry cranes, brass furnace, powerful crab, two sets of shear legs, set of four 10-inch pulley blocks, 90 yards new chain for ditto, Pooley's patent weighing machine to weigh 10cwt., valuable brass force pump, anvils, smith's bellows, large quantity of new cast iron factory windows, large quantity of smith's and fitter's tools, foundry ladles, large loom carriage and wrought iron railway, the whole of the gas fittings.

What a host of skilled activities and associated noises in varied spaces this list conjures up!

There was another Silk Mill on the market in February 1867. This would be a frequent happening in later Victorian times in Derby as the competition of imported foreign products at lower prices bit hard. Chancellors of the Exchequer beginning with Gladstone were believers in free trade and so cut or cancelled altogether the customs duties from abroad. In this case Thomas Peake of Abbey Street was getting rid of a 'small convenient Silk Throwing Mill' which was also 'now in full work', a phrase suggestive of lay-offs being perhaps a frequent occurrence. It had two rooms only, with 1,600 spindles in one of them and also 'doubling, drawing, and reeling machines'. The reference to full production going on at this mill at this particular time also seems to contrast conspicuously with an impression of doom and gloom in the textile industry in Derby in other reports from later on in the century. In January 1878 the *Mercury* reported that the South Scotland Chamber of Commerce meeting at Hawick refused to back complaints about foreign competition from Derby cotton mill bosses. When a certain 'Mr Laing' had asked to look around one of the Derby cotton mills he had been told 'that nobody would get into that factory, as everything in it was about two generations old'. The Scots had concluded that Derby mills should pull themselves up by their own boot laces. But in January 1897 the *Mercury* was again reporting that a Derby man (Mr G.B. Unsworth), who was presumably a mill boss, told the Silk Association Council that there would soon be 'not a manufacturer in the town' despite its being 'the birthplace of the English silk industry'. He added that 'machinery was being sold at old iron prices'. Japanese and French competition were specifically mentioned as being responsible for this dire state of affairs.

The iron trade seems to have been more successful in what was really the age of steam and rail. In October 1867 James Haywood, boss of the Phoenix Foundry on the opposite bank of the river to the Old Silk Mill, was congratulated by the engineers of the London and Brighton Railway for the 'very satisfactory manner in which Mr H. carried out the great and difficult work entrusted to him'. The Pheonix firm had constructed a bridge at Battersea carrying 'several lines of railway without obstruction to the traffic' in order to 'improve the access to the Victoria station'.

Capital of industry

The supreme success story of Derby's Victorian industry, the raft upon which so many other enterprises floated, was the Midland Railway itself. Around its classically fronted station were grouped its workshops, its offices, its turntable house, its hotel, its clubhouse and even its engine-drivers' terraces. In February 1856 the *Mercury* reported on the Railway's most recent Board meeting, at which the chairman, Mr John Ellis, presented 'what, to his mind, was the most satisfactory report that had ever been presented to them since he had had the honour of occupying his present position'. Of course, the capitalist 'project' was based on a gospel of competition and struggle in which the fittest survived. Mr Ellis also announced that the Company's shareholders were to have their dividend halved from 7 to 3 3/4 percent. New heavy engines had to be bought to replace ageing four-wheeled stock that a Government inspector considered unsafe and the Company had also had to cope with the 'aggressive policy' of their rivals the Great Northern. The latter, as we have seen, would thrust into the middle of Derby by 1878.

The Midland would continue to expand in spite of the competition. A reflective *Mercury* paragraph in August 1888 announced the Company's acquisition of Osmaston Park on the south-eastern edge of town beyond the Pullman coach construction sheds. Old Osmaston Hall had long been abandoned to the encroaching racket and smoke of industry and new housing

The Sharon Chemical Company's Works, 1894, a painting by A.J. Keene of part of the industrial scene on the Chester Green side of the Derwent. These works were on the Mansfield Road beside the Little Eaton branch of the Derby Canal. An abundance of smoke accompanies the tower of All Saints' in the near distance. (Courtesy: Derby Museums and Art Gallery)

estates had closed in on its grounds on the eastern side. But under Midland ownership, the reporter was confident that 'the prospective loss of what used to be – and is now when the wind blows the smoke any other way – a very pleasant walk' would be compensated for by added prosperity for the town and enhanced property values round about!

However, the Derby skilled worker could well find employment for his/her talents in scores of smaller firms, one of which was the subject of praise in a *Mercury* article in November 1897. Eastwood's tannery in Full Street dated back to the middle of the 18th century. It prided itself in turning out high-quality leather in the old way – the only bit of machinery in the place was for 'grinding bark and pumping the liquor', whatever that might mean. At any rate, members of the royal family had featured among its customers!

Joys and cares of ownership

It was customary for the bosses of larger industrial enterprises to show their appreciation of their workforce with an annual outing. So in August 1867 the 250 and more employees of Bath Street Elastic Works were able to spend a summer's day in gorgeous Dovedale at Mr G. Holme's expense. After gathering for their horse-drawn transport in front of nearby St Helen's House (Derby School), to be entertained on the journey by the Band of the First Derbyshire Volunteers, they duly arrived in the dale to follow their own fancy, some to scramble up rugged Thorpe Cloud, others to stroll alongside the river itself. Then they danced to the strains of the band, sat down to 'a sumptuous dinner, consisting of every delicacy' in a large tent, enjoyed 'various amusements until five o'clock' and finally returned to the tent for 'a splendid tea'.

In contrast to that picture of complete harmony, other company occasions took place rather in the shadow of possible conflict between master and worker. In December 1866 Messrs

Swingler and Son, large-scale manufacturers of iron at Litchurch, gave a dinner at the County Hotel to 'nearly 300 men and boys' who earlier that year had defied a Trade Union call for strike action. To keep production going the management had brought in 'Non-Unionists, principally from Staffordshire'. Several after-dinner speeches, no doubt much to the delight of the *Mercury*'s editor, referred to 'the abominable tyranny of the Trades-Unionists' and a Town Councillor expressed his pleasure at seeing 'unity between masters and men' that evening with the result that 'the interests of the town must be largely promoted'. The Chairman (Director) urged his employees to subscribe to sick clubs for insurance against accident or sickness rather than the sort of Union that 'takes a man's money and shuts him out of work when he would rather be in it'.

The façade of Haslam's Union Mills, all that is left today of the enterprise that produced the first ever ship refrigeration unit and provided major employment for Chester Green after Haslam took over and considerably extended the original 20-year-old mill. (Photo: Andrew Butterton)

Again, in August 1897 a reference to strikes was made at an event arranged by the boss of another of the town's major industrial enterprises, Haslam's Union Mills at Chester Green. Nearly 20 years earlier these mills had produced the first refrigeration equipment for ocean-going vessels and so opened the way for large-scale importing of meat from the Antipodes and the Americas. Sir Alfred Haslam, knighted by the Queen on her visit to Derby in 1891, and Lady Haslam took no fewer than 800 of their employees by special train to Matlock Bath to celebrate the coming of age of their son Alfred Victor. Apart from the far-famed beauties of the place, the huge company enjoyed the playing of the Matlock Band outside the Pavilion, various sports and finally tea in the building itself. In his speech Sir Alfred:

> ...referred to the distressful relations existing at the present time between employers and employed, and said that a great struggle was going on in respect to the eight hours [a day] movement. Happily the strike had not extended to their industry, and they might well rejoice in that fact (Applause). He hoped that a time would arrive when a better understanding would prevail among the masters and men.

There was no doubting where the editor of the *Mercury*'s sympathies lay on the issue. In December 1897 he penned a glowing obituary for another of the prominent town bosses, Sir John Smith. He was head of a brass founding firm in St Mary's Gate that had done well out of the Crimean War as an Admiralty supplier. On the basis of this firm footing he had become a respected town Councillor, then Mayor and Alderman. The Prince of Wales (soon to become King Edward VII) thought much of him, though he was:

> ... not a brilliant man, or gifted with the arts and graces of speech; he was simply a plain, honest citizen who always ran a straight course, whose ideas were understandable by everybody... Sir John as a link with the Derby of half a century ago was, perhaps, the best authority left to us. He remembered the old rowing club days, and the old political and municipal days, and the old ways of doing things which our forefathers practised.

Hugely respected, he loved his native town and 'no man could talk about old Derby better than Sir John Smith, and no man was prouder of the strides forward it has made than he'.

CHAPTER 7

Up Before the Beak

DERBYSHIRE SPRING ASSIZES. Yesterday about three o'clock, Edward A. Holden, Esq. the High Sheriff of the county, after entertaining his friends at Ashton Hall, entered the town accompanied by a numerous and highly respectable cavalcade, and immediately proceeded to meet the Judge of Assize at Chaddesden.

(*Derby Mercury*, 14 March 1838)

What a cosy little affair! Before the age of television, which might take as its motto Thomas Cranmer's memorable old Prayer Book clause 'from whom no secrets are hid', people set up in authority over others had unchallenged opportunity to build and command respect for law and hierarchy and at the same time bolster and show off their status as the guardians of the 'status quo', things as they were and perhaps always had been. They applied the law and 'dished it out'! Derby, as the county town of Derbyshire, enclosed within its boundaries County Hall in St Mary's Gate. Inside its stately 17th-century stone walls, with their multi-paned round-topped windows and balustraded roof, the Queen's judges from London presided four times a year over the higher law courts known as Assizes. The importance of these occasions as the means by which the ruler's authority, supported by the section of society that owned most of the land, was exercised against the people who upset her peace, was underlined by the way in which the judges entered town. They were met by the High Sheriff of Derbyshire and a posse of the most important locals, as in 1838. In those days, respect was indeed all.

There was, apparently, a lowering of expected standards in the early 1860s as in March 1867 the *Times of London* noted that the High Sheriff that year met 'Mr Justice Lush' with a posse 'the elegance of which showed that the present holder of that office is not unmindful of the respect due to Her Majesty's representatives'. So normal service had obviously been resumed. Back in July 1846 for the Summer Assizes, the *Mercury* reported that the reception group, 'a large party of gentlemen', were entertained to a breakfast that 'included every delicacy' at

County (Shire) Hall, St Mary's Gate, before its recent restoration. The handsome 17th-century building was the setting for the county's legal ceremonial and for Derby's major Victorian courtroom dramas. (Photo: Dr Frank Jones)

Osmaston Hall, the home of the High Sheriff for that year Sir Robert Wilmot, before meeting the Judges two miles from town on the Osmaston Road. The Hall had not yet fallen into the giant clutches of the Midland Railway and was still obviously a family home. For the procession to St Mary's Gate they were joined by 'a number of the tradesmen of Derby and agriculturalists [farmers] of the neighbourhood'.

There was an altogether grander affair in March 1856 when the High Sheriff was one of the Mundy family of Shipley Hall to the north. For this occasion he had issued 'a general invitation to his friends and tenantry to partake of his hospitality' so that in spite of the rain 'upwards of 200 guests were assembled at his beautiful seat' for the breakfast that again, in a time-honoured *Mercury* phrase, 'included every delicacy'. Of course the tenants took their repast in a separate room from the 'friends'. Leaving for Derby, the procession consisted of 'two trumpeters (Mr Hunt and Mr Ratcliffe), twenty javelin men, two abreast, on horseback, the high sheriff's carriage, the officers of the court and many gentlemen of the county and town in carriages and on horseback'. Fanfares were blown at 'Smalley, Morley, and other places on the line of route' and there were lots of spectators on hand that afternoon to appreciate the show. The precise destination this time was the Railway Station, since their Lordships the judges now came from London by rail. They would then have mounted the Sheriff's dress coach, 'a very handsomely appointed vehicle' supplied by Messrs Holmes of London Road, to ride through Derby streets to County Hall. In 1867, in amends for the previous year's alleged meanness, 'Her Majesty's Judges' were provided with a 'splendidly appointed carriage and attendants in suitable liveries' and the High Sheriff had '50 or 60 horsemen' with him to welcome the proud visitors.

When the opening ceremony at County Hall was over there would be another short procession the length of St Mary's Gate to the doors of All Saints' for 'Divine Service' and later a hotel dinner. In July 1846 the 'learned Judges' and company listened to 'an extremely able and appropriate sermon' preached by the Sheriff's chaplain, presumably a vicar not far from Shipley, as the corresponding 'impressive discourse' in March 1856 was, according to the *Mercury,* given by the 'Incumbent [parish priest] of Cotmanhay'. That year, too, the dinner was at the Bell Hotel and included of course 'every delicacy in season, and was served in an excellent manner'. In March 1867 the dining took place at the King's Head Hotel, the meal 'a very excellent one, and the service of crystal had a very beautiful effect'.

Inside court

Assizes began with a speech by the chief judge to the Grand Jury, who had the responsibility of deciding on the verdict in the cases to be heard. This speech was in the form of a report about the state of the law in the county of Derbyshire. So in November 1899 Mr Justice Channel drew the jury's attention to the fact that in Derbyshire crimes against women and children (domestic violence) were increasing while 'crime figures in general were decreasing'. He also thought that the popular response to such crimes, which was to flog the culprits, was not as effective as enabling 'an improvement in the conditions of life of the class from which most offenders came'. Haven't we heard that before, with equal justice, much more recently? The *Mercury*'s editor commented on the crime figures that the increase in domestic violence cases might be due to more education and therefore 'increased public sensitivity' leading to more reporting of such cases than in earlier times.

Then came the judging. Victorian judges operated a much more humane system than their 18th-century predecessors, who protected property that might seem to us now worth next to nothing with the threat of the death penalty for anyone tempted to go for it. This was largely due to the work of Sir Robert Peel, a reforming Home Secretary of the 1820s. So when Noah Foster, aged 15, Ralph Fowler Ketland, aged 16, and James Wilkinson, aged 17, came before the judge at County Hall at the Derbyshire Summer Assizes on 29 July 1846 charged with stealing 'one goose, the property of Daniel Hunt', his lordship ordered them to be 'imprisoned for the space of one month'. The three lads, who were undefended, were described as:

... ironstone getters from Staffordshire, and were seeking work. They had picked up prosecutor's goose, which appeared to have been straying on the turnpike road, and on its being traced to them they gave contradictory accounts of its possession. Mary Pickering, aunt of Foster, who said she had travelled 50 miles to speak for him, gave him a good character, and spoke favourably as far as her knowledge extended of the other two prisoners.

The judge gave them a lecture about serious crime having a habit of developing out of trivial first offences and warned them they could face transportation if they offended again. This was a punishment, being packed off to Australia for seven to 14 years and therefore savage enough to us now, that had become the favoured substitute for the death penalty during the early part of the century. The *Mercury* had reported a sad case of its application in April 1838:

> On the night of Friday last, a prisoner, of the name of William Gaunt, aged 22 years, who was under sentence of transportation, having been tried at the last assizes and convicted of horse stealing, committed suicide in our county gaol. It appeared that the deceased hung himself by suspending himself by means of his neck-cloth to the upper hinge of the door which closes the window of his cell.

Transportation in turn had disappeared off the punishment menu by 1870.

More serious than theft was surely an episode in September 1856 after the end of the Crimean War, which also provides us with a reminder of Derby's intimate connection with its surrounding countryside. Another threesome, David, James and Francis Ault, were charged with assaulting a Derby policeman who had been ordered to arrest another member of the same family, Charles, for deserting the Army. The officer was accompanied by a waggoner from Longford and his dog and had caught up with Charles Ault in a field near the village of Rodsley. The other three went for the policeman, 'struck him several times, and then armed themselves with sickles and used threatening language'. Charles Ault escaped. The three defendants were labourers for the farmer who owned the field and what he had to say in court 'did not tend to exonerate his reapers'. They were therefore 'convicted in the penalty of £1 each and costs, or six weeks' imprisonment', which would seem to be evidence of the law becoming yet more lenient as the consensus in the Court was 'that this was a very bad case'.

Repeat offenders could make County Hall judges angry and therefore harsher, as in July 1867: 'William Gibson, 14, was sent to gaol for two months with hard labour, and while there to receive 20 lashes, for stealing a chemise and a pair of garters, the property of Mary Ann Haines and Mrs Marshall, at Litchurch. He had been many times previously convicted.' Some weeks earlier in May a case in another dimension altogether was tried at County Hall, which surely revealed the depths of wretchedness that existed in some, perhaps many, poverty-stricken homes in mean terraced streets. Joseph Darwin, 'a little lad with an intelligent face', appeared before the Bench with his mother, 'a sickly-looking untidy woman'. They were from Peel Street, Litchurch, which was until 1877 separate from Derby and part of the county. This was why they were present in St Mary's Gate rather than the Borough Police Court, and in the company of a Superintendent of the County Constabulary. His investigating officer went on to

The County Gaol, Vernon Street, built in 1826. For many of those condemned at County Hall it was the place of their confinement, while for some it was their last resting place, with executions taking place to the right of the entrance. The street would be crowded with watchers for the tell-tale black smoke to rise above the battlements until the 1860s. (Photo: Andrew Butterton)

relate the sad details the magistrates needed to hear. The woman and her husband, in the phrase used in the *Mercury* report of the case, were convicted of 'gross inhumanity' to their son. The constable created a sensation in court when he produced a huge stone with a hole in the middle and a heavy cart-chain through it joined with a smaller chain with a padlock at one end. This was the object he had discovered on entering the house on Peel Street after a tip-off. The apparatus was attached to the boy round his stomach, cutting into his skin so that he might have died if the policeman had not freed him after calling for a man with a pair of pincers. In addition the Court was shown large bruises on the boy's back. These had been caused by his father beating him with 'a bit of a whip stop' that morning, because 'he goes out from morning to night and stops out all night at times. I have tried him in all manner of ways.' The same reason was given by the mother for chaining him. A neighbour said the boy 'had been chained about a fortnight, day after day, and he was frequently beaten, his cries being most heartrending'. After the Chairman of the Bench had declared that 'We have never had a case brought before us of a more brutal character than this', he sentenced the father, who said he worked as a labourer at the railway station, to three months' hard labour. The boy's mother left the Court saying 'she should have to go into the workhouse now that her husband had gone'.

In August 1888 a sentence of execution was arrived at by the jury at County Hall in just 10 minutes, according to the *Mercury*. The Derbyshire Summer Assizes had heard the case of Arthur Thomas Delaney, a 31-year-old fitter, and had convicted him of the murder of his wife at their cottage in Chesterfield on 21 April that year after a night out at their local, the Red Lion. The consequence was that the final moments of the tragic story took place about half a mile away from County Hall inside the grim compound of the County Gaol in Vernon Street. Delaney was the seventh person to be executed in Derby since Victoria became Queen, the previous occasion having been eight years earlier. The scaffold was put up 'against the outer wall of the prison on the right hand side of the main entrance'. Something new since that previous execution was 'a covering placed over it in order to shut off the view of some portion of the proceedings which would otherwise be possible from the roofs of some neighbouring houses'. The end came at eight o'clock on a fine summer's morning after the prisoner had been marched briskly between two warders to the grim shed, the chaplain in front reciting sentences from the burial service, not noticing the grave 'which had already been dug for him next to those of the other murderers who have expiated their crimes in the prison'. The chapel bell had tolled for over a quarter of an hour when the crowd outside filling Vernon Street 'and the other thoroughfares adjacent to the prison' heard a dull thud and saw the black flag hoisted to confirm that execution had indeed taken place. Some of the spectators were reported to have walked from Chesterfield for this moment.

At the local

While County Hall in St Mary's Gate was the venue for important judicial scenes at three-monthly intervals, the Borough Police Court at the Guildhall was in action week-in, week-out for a whole range of petty and sometimes not-so-petty cases. Theft was a staple of course, as in a case reported in January 1856 when 18-year-old factory hand Margaret Tatum was charged with stealing 'a blanket, a shawl, a victorine, a bonnet, and various other articles' from a widow at Litchurch. The girl had been employed to do odd jobs in the house. However, the owner asked that the Bench show mercy and the girl got two months' imprisonment. More mercy was shown a fortnight earlier to 13-year-old William Taylor, who was charged with 'various petty robberies' by a man in Uttoxeter Road who had employed him to run errands. The local constable said 'the lad was a very bad one', he had often stolen before and was used to getting rid of objects at a place in Sadler Gate with a sign over the door promising 'Money advanced on any property consigned for sale'. Since the employer didn't want to press charges the lad was 'remanded, and subsequently discharged'.

There was an even more positive outcome in a case that September when Mary Wilson, 'a pitiable looking woman' from Nottinghamshire, was charged with stealing 'dolly pegs' from a woman in Lodge Lane and selling them again in Sadler Gate, though at a different shop. Once more the owner of the pegs decided not to press charges and the magistrates ordered Mary's rail fare to Nottingham to be paid by the Court after she had told them 'she had slept in the fields at the outskirts of the town for several nights, and had no prospect of getting work'.

While occasional waves of theft could be put down to well-known offenders, like the one on the Rose Hill Estate reported in the first edition of the *Mercury* for 1856, in which two youths faced three indictments for breaking into summer houses over several weeks 'stealing garden tools, fenders, fire irons, saws, planes and other articles', other cases underline an impression of hopeless misery as the motive for petty wrongdoing. In December 1888 Maria Brown 'who carried a baby', pleaded guilty to stealing '25 broaches, 13 pendants, a number of paper knives, and other small articles, of the value together of £2.10s,' from a shop on Osmaston Road. Her husband was in gaol for a month for stealing handkerchiefs and she in turn was sentenced to 14 days' hard labour. Mrs Churchill, the keeper of the lodging house where Maria lived, agreed to look after the baby 'which had been crowing merrily in the dock during the hearing of the case' so that it would not have to be put into the workhouse.

At times, especially it seems with boys, whom perhaps they thought might be put off acquiring a crime habit, magistrates could hand out physical punishment. In August 1856 a boy who 'received a bad character' was ordered to be flogged for stealing one shilling from a house in Upper Brook Street.

Kaleidoscope of wrong-doing

Not surprisingly, with a choice of about 170 hotels, taverns, pubs and licensed premises to choose from in 1837 and no fewer than 574 by 1897, drunks were frequently to be seen in front of the beak in Derby. Sadly some of these were women, as we have already glimpsed when surveying the street scene. Vintage year 1856 saw assorted public nuisance-doing all over the town. In January a 'hawker of hats' from Walker Lane was locked up after one of his regular disturbing visits to the Old Tiger Inn, where according to the landlord 'when told that the company did not want any of his goods commenced being abusive and used threatening language'. He was freed after promising not to go near there again. In July two young women 'whose appearance was more respectable than their conduct' were locked up for violently ringing the bell of the Royal Hotel right in the centre of town at 'about a quarter to one that morning'. This was something that the arresting officer said was often done in order to get a servant to open the door and find nothing! Both of the women were drunk and one of them 'used the most disgusting and indecent language which it was possible for a woman to do'. She received 14 days' hard labour for her efforts while her companion, who had actually rung the bell, got off with a five-shilling fine.

During the same month a labourer named William Taylor got a month's gaol for running away from Derby leaving his two young children in an empty house in St James's Lane to be looked after by the parish (St Peter's). He had been picked up in Nottingham, having already done a similar thing the previous year, running off with a woman who had left five children with Shardlow parish.

But it was in December that the most distinctive incident in our selection of misdemeanors in Victorian Derby took place. In fact, as the *Mercury* reporter saw it, there was indeed technically no wrong-doing in the case, simply an example of alert anticipation on the part of 'The Force' combined with a general sense of guilt on the part of their quarry! The newspaper

The Royal Hotel, target of nuisance activity in 1856. In the distance on the left is the tower and spire of Victoria Street Congregational Church, the place of worship of several Aldermen of the Council and now replaced by a modern structure. The photograph dates from 1896. (Courtesy: Derby Museums and Art Gallery)

headed the story 'An Aquatic Thief' and it was all about the consequences of two officers of the Derby police deciding to do a Friday evening check on a report that a gang of thieves had recently come into the town and had taken up residence 'in various low public houses'. The officers soon had in their hands a purse containing three sovereigns which a 'showily dressed woman' in company with two men had allegedly abandoned on sight of 'the Law'. However, the lady in question successfully made an application through a solicitor for the return of the purse as she claimed the money was her own 'hard earnings' from selling caps.

Whether they were the same individuals as were seen with her earlier is unclear, but a 'party' was reported loitering in Full Street to hear the result of her request. On seeing two other police officers coming towards them, one of the party, described as 'a well-dressed "swellish" looking man', dashed off. 'By way of a joke' the policemen gave chase. They were getting near him by St Michael's Church so he 'bolted down the lane', as a stranger to Derby not realising that at the end there was simply a wall and on the other side of that the river! He went over, crossing the weir of the Old Silk Mill to arrive at the Phoenix foundry on the other side of the river. However, there was a brawny reception committee on the bank so the fugitive 'again took to the water, and succeeded in landing in the late Mr Mousley's grounds and getting clear away'. Of course, the scene caused the officers 'much merriment' despite the failure of the chase.

There was no doubting the offence that came before the Borough Court during the last week of 1877. A 13-year-old girl from Bag Lane, 'of rather diminutive stature' according to

George Twigden's gondola ride at Derby Fair in the Morledge, probably in the 1890s. The engine had 11 moving figures in front, which during the Boer War were given generals' heads! (Courtesy: Derby Local Studies Library)

the *Mercury* reporter, was violently assaulted in Thorntree Lane. On a night off from her job 'in service at No. 12, Abbey Street', she went with friends to the shooting galleries in the Morledge. When she refused to have a drink with her assailant and turned away he 'ran after her and caught hold of her, and then dragged her by the neck'. A woman who lived in Thorntree Square heard a scream and on going out into the lane found the girl and the accused running off. The girl claimed he had tried to rape her. The woman gave chase, the man went into the Castle pub, she waited for him to come out again, and when he did so he 'used the most disgusting language'. The Court heard that he had been 'repeatedly punished for assaulting women' and gave him six months' hard labour.

In October 1878 a similar offence in a more long-drawn-out form in a domestic setting was tried in the Borough Court and reported on at length in the *Mercury*. It surely reveals the reality of who possessed power in the family in Victorian times and also the temptations this power led to in the setting of lower-middle-class household relationships. A coal merchant of No.6, Oxford Terrace, Osmaston Road, was charged with raping his 14-year-old servant girl on 9 October. It was obviously a *cause celebre* in the town when the prosecutor declared that 'it was a matter of considerable regret to him, and it must be to everyone in the Court, that a man occupying so respectable a position in the town as did the defendant should be in the position in which he now stood'. Five minutes after his wife and her sister from Nottingham had gone out after having a cup of tea in the dining room looking out to the garden at the back, the husband entered through the front door. The girl had gone down to the kitchen with the couple's little daughter. After also being served tea in the dining room, the master went down to the kitchen and started molesting the servant girl, pursuing her up and down the stairs between dining room and kitchen while she attempted to clear and wash up. In the phrase used at that time he 'had connection with her' three times while she screamed. When his wife returned for a few minutes he disappeared into the back yard. He came back in when his wife went out of the front door again and tried to convince the girl that there would be trouble if she told anyone about what had happened. When she replied 'I shall tell my brother', he told her that he had 'served another girl like that' but she was not to worry if his wife spoke sharply to her: 'Don't take any notice of her'. When he took his wife out that evening the girl was told that she must on no account go out but an errand the following afternoon gave her the excuse to call at a friend's house in Litchurch Street and tell her what had taken place. Later on the girl also told her sister when she asked the mistress for permission to get some more clothes. That night she went to see a surgeon who confirmed evidence of sexual interference later in Court and then went on to the police-station.

The court appearance resulted in the coal-merchant being committed to appear at the Winter Assizes in St Mary's Gate three weeks later on 31 October. However, judgment was deferred to the following Derby Assizes when the jury failed to reach a verdict after being out for an hour and a half. Since the surgeon had testified that 'there were no marks of violence, such as would have been expected were it against the girl's consent', the charge was lowered to one of indecent assault.

The very next month the Court sat in judgment on a different and sadly frequent kind of assault case, an example of domestic violence within the family. A man was charged with assaulting and beating his wife. He was given a month's hard labour, double the ration he had received for the same offence three years earlier, though his wife admitted that she was now living with one of his employees. According to the *Mercury* report she:

> ... said on the 3 January she was in the Beech Tree public house talking to the prisoner's cousin, who comes from Nottingham, when the prisoner, who had left her two years before, came in, and taking up a glass he struck her several times with it, and then threw it at her. She was taken to the Infirmary, and had suffered greatly from the attack; seven pieces of glass had been taken out of her head, and she suffered very much now every time there was a change of weather.

An example of a variation on this admittedly depressing theme was the subject of a case in February 1897. According to the *Mercury* 'Sarah Reeves, of 3, Goodwin Street, was summoned for assaulting Elizabeth Hooton, of 5, Goodwin Street', who was also 'charged with assaulting Reeves' daughter, Mary Jane Mills'. Reeves was fined 10s and costs or 14 days in gaol for allegedly rushing into her neighbour's house with her daughter, striking Hooton 'several times over the head with a key, which stunned her'. They then 'hit her in the eye, blacking it, and they dragged her about the floor by the hair of her head'. The reason for this behaviour, according to Hooton, was that 'she would not lend Reeves any more money for drink'. Reeves in turn argued that she had been provoked and anyway had 'only hit the woman once with her fist'. The Bench dismissed a counter-summons on Hooton for allegedly running 'full kick' at Mills and throwing a knife at her. Both methods of attack had missed the target!

There was another, sadly frequent, type of crime before the Court in May 1897. By this time there was in existence a Derbyshire branch of the Royal Society for the Prevention of Cruelty to Animals, which had obtained 168 convictions the previous year. The useful and willing horse was often the victim of the Victorian version of man's dominion over animal life. Two men from Brook Street, Derby, were charged with cruelty to a gelding through overloading it. One witness, an employee of the Derby Tramways Company, reported seeing one of the men 'in charge of two horses and carts on the Uttoxeter New Road' and one of the animals had seemed tired. Another witness, a JP from Mickleover, related that as he was going home on the afternoon in question 'he heard a crash, and a little later that one of the animals had fallen down. It seemed exhausted, and was apparently in great pain. It was cut about the eye, and when extricated from the shafts fell down again. It was in a pitiable condition.' A police sergeant testified that there were nearly two tons of coal in the cart and when an inspector visited the accused's stables 'the man met him with a volley of abuse, and ordered him off the premises. He acted like a madman, but witness eventually got to see the gelding. It was in a terrible state, and was in slings. It appeared as if it was going to die, and there was a very large lump on its eye. It was cut about the knees, and lock-jaw set in, with the result that it had had to be killed.' The owner had been 10 times convicted of similar offences. He was fined £2 plus costs or 21 days' hard labour.

A Midland Railway locomotive, a product of their workshops in November 1883, taken by the company's official photographer Thomas Cotton. (Courtesy: Derby Museums and Art Gallery)

Finally, in our selected menu from the Borough Police Court proceedings, an example of the most serious crime of all, murder. In early December 1900 William Wopling, a single 35-year-old employee of the Midland Railway Carriage Works, who had come up to Derby from the village of Toosey in Essex where he had been born and had worked as a farm labourer, was charged with killing his 54-year-old widowed landlady Mary Jane Moore. They had lived at 99 Graham Street, where the tragic incident had allegedly taken place one Saturday evening. Wopling had come in early before 8pm 'somewhat the worse for drink' after an afternoon in town. He refused to eat the supper put before him, there followed an argument with Mrs Moore and he was then said to have assaulted her, 'cutting her in the face'. Mrs Moore asked him why he didn't leave because 'she did not want him in the house any longer!' She turned to go to the kitchen to wash her hands when it is alleged Wopling 'threw a lighted lamp at her, and her clothing became ignited. She tried to extinguish the flames but failed, and ran into the garden where neighbours came to her assistance. The flames were eventually extinguished and she was conveyed to the Infirmary'. The house-surgeon telephoned the police when he saw her condition. When they got to Graham Street 'Wopling was half-dressed in bed, still the worse for drink'. The subsequent Coroner's jury 'found him guilty of murder and committed him for trial at the Assizes'.

The Force and its enemies

The Derby Borough Police Force started in 1835, two years before Victoria became Queen. It had eight constables who earned 15–18s a week, supported by 10 watchmen for night duty. By 1846 a superintendent with a salary of '£150 a year, with a house' had been appointed and the number of constables had increased to 20. From 1856 there were four sergeants and 25 constables. In March 1867 they were in need of new uniforms, judging by an advertisement in the *Mercury* from the Town Hall requesting 'Sealed and endorsed Tenders' to supply '43 SUITS OF UNIFORM CLOTHING for the Derby Borough Police' to be delivered within a month. Traders interested could 'inspect a sample suit on application to Mr Hilton, Head Constable'.

Their command of the streets did not go unchallenged. In November 1837 the *Mercury* reported that the watchmen in particular faced difficulties and had 'repeatedly complained, that when disturbances in the street took place, successful opposition from bodies of young men who rescued offenders, was a frequent practice'. By 1856 the *Mercury* was reporting violence against constables themselves. That January a seemingly vicious inhabitant of River Street, when asked by a constable who had followed him about 11 o'clock at night from the top of Well Street what he was doing 'getting over a high wall of Mr Sherwin's orchard in St Helen's Street', replied that 'it was no business of his [the constable's], neither would he tell his name nor where he resided'. On being taken to the lock-up 'he was very rough, struck, bit, and kicked him, and lamed him by stamping on his toes'. Another constable managed to get to his colleague, now on the ground with the prisoner, and when he in turn tried to intervene was also badly kicked and struck!

In November the same year there was the latest of a long sequence of incidents with a certain character, Thomas Byrom, who seems to have had absolutely no fear of or regard for the Borough police. A constable had been called in to the Star and Garter on a Sunday evening to be faced by Byrom 'stripped and wanting to fight'. On being challenged he punched the policeman in the mouth. When the two went down on the floor together 'the prisoner was rescued by a number of Irishmen'. The landlord testified against him and the Bench dished out 'the full penalty of £5 or one month's imprisonment'.

On the other hand, there could be at least a smidgen of sympathy for those who had broken

Looking up Well Street from St Alkmund's Well, the scene of an on-going violent confrontation with the Law in 1856. (Photo: Andrew Butterton)

the law. In the harsh world of early Victorian sentencing policy, the *Mercury* reported in 1838 on what must have been one of the occasional sad processions through the town by coach or after 1840 to or from the railway station: 'On Friday morning last, C. Potter (and child), H. Brown, and S. Dan, female convicts, were removed from our county gaol to be placed on board the female convict ship at Woolwich, until their several terms of transportation can be carried into effect'. In June 1888 there was indeed no attempt to disguise the reporter's feelings:

> That was not a pretty sight which was witnessed in Friar Gate last Tuesday evening – three men and a boy, apparently of 14, chained together, on their way from the station to the prison, crawling along at the slowest pace to accommodate a fifth prisoner, an old man whose legs could scarcely carry him. These unhappy people had doubtless broken the law of their country, and deserved to go to prison, but we are rather dubious that it was ever contemplated that part of their punishment should consist of being dragged a mile and a half through the streets of a town, handcuffed and shackled, for the amusement of a crowd of little boys, and to the disgust of decent people.

However, this was hardly the responsibility of the Derby Borough Police Force, which seems to have carried out its duties, on the evidence of some of the cases we have observed, with humanity and indeed humour, despite the trials and provocations of the really difficult characters who crossed its path.

CHAPTER 8

On Behalf of the Community

BOROUGH POLICE COURT, MONDAY. Mr Thos. Stenson, a member of the Derby Town Council, was summoned by James Dickens, a bill-sticker, for having on Wednesday, the 20th ult., kicked the side of his paste-can in, upset his paste, and deprived him of a number of bills confided to his charge for circulation, thereby committing damage to the amount of 2s.6d. – The complainant stated that he was employed by Mr Geo. Keys, a bill-poster, and on the morning of Wednesday last, he was about to paste one of Cox and Harpur's [Tory] bills opposite to the defendant's house, when the defendant came up to him and threatened to kick him, and he said he should kick the bucket over too (a laugh). The bucket – a zinc one – having been produced, with a deep indentation on its side, the complainant continued: the bucket was on the floor, and I had got my brush in the centre of Cox and Harpur's paper, and was going to put it on the wall; he said if I did not take the bill down he would kick the bucket over; I did not take it down, and he kicked it over, and when all the 'stuff' had run out he kicked the bucket into the middle of the road.

(*Derby Mercury*, 6 November 1867)

Party political feelings could run high, then as now, when election time came round. Who should run the town and be Councillors? Who should run the country and be Members of Parliament, Liberals (otherwise known as Radicals to their opponents), Conservatives (Tories to the other side) or, right at the end of the century, Labourites (Socialists to those who did not wish them well)? Councillor Stenson was Liberal, as Derby tended to be in Victorian times, did not appear in court on this occasion and was ordered to pay costs or take seven days in gaol. Again, then as now, passions were fiercest when the big issues affecting everyone in the country in some way were at stake in a General Election.

Political battle

There was a General Election soon after Victoria took up sole residence at Buckingham Palace. In July 1837 the *Mercury* commented on the 'bustle and excitement' in the town because of it. There was no secret ballot until the 1870s. In those days the candidates were introduced in person to those comparatively few citizens who had the vote at the Guildhall in the Market Place on the day before the casting of votes took place. Five years earlier Parliament had agreed to a Reform Bill that gave more people the vote, but still left out people who merely rented their homes rather than owned them. So the workers of the town still had no choice of government. According to Glover's 1833 *History and Gazetteer of Derby*, 1,500 people now had the vote out of a total population of 21,000! Still, when the Guildhall gates were opened at 10 o'clock on the Monday, 'it was almost instantly filled to an almost intolerable excess; and it became apparent that great uproar and disturbance were to be expected'. In fact, when the speeches were made, the man who introduced Edward Strutt, candidate for the Liberals, accused the Tories of dirty tricks, of trying to set 'the workman against the manufacturer' and of attacking the new Poor Law and workhouses brought in by the Liberal government. He was the last man able to get himself heard! The one who introduced Strutt's side-kick, the Hon. Mr Ponsonby, was 'received with cheers and groans', and when it was the turn of the Hon. Francis Curzon, the Tory candidate, to be introduced, the speaker registered 'scarcely more than a word at a time'. When another speaker ventured his support he 'was entirely prevented from attempting any address to the meeting'. It got worse! When Strutt himself tried to speak 'it was impossible to catch more than a sentence at a time, and that at considerable intervals'. Ponsonby was 'more imperfectly heard than any previous speaker'. Curzon got 'cheering from one party and groans from the other' and his companion Colville faced 'continued uproar'.

When the Mayor asked for a show of hands, the numbers raised for both parties seemed so close that both claimed victory. On a second showing the Mayor gave it to the Liberals but the Tories refused to accept it and not unreasonably demanded a proper count, which was fixed for the next day, Tuesday. Voting took place from 8am to 4pm and Strutt and Ponsonby were returned to Parliament by majorities of over 300 each.

It isn't often that church bells are rung to celebrate happenings in politics but they were in Derby in June 1846. The towers of St Alkmund's and St Michael's rang out one Friday morning, not for an election but for an extreme example of the sort of thing that takes place at Westminster as the result of one. Just as the Health Service has been a mighty political football in recent years, so in the early 1840s were what were known as the Corn Laws. These rules had been passed by Parliament 30 years earlier at a time before the Reform Bill when it was controlled by landowners and farmers. These rules kept the price of wheat artificially high by preventing cheaper corn from abroad being brought in unless the price of English-grown wheat went above a certain level. The farmers in the lovely country around Derby would be all in favour of the Corn Laws. The people of Derby, bosses and workers alike, would mostly want them cancelled (repealed) so that bread could become cheaper. The Tory Prime Minister of the early 1840s, Sir Robert Peel, himself from a factory-owning family, enraged his supporters by taking on board the campaign to get the Corn Laws cancelled. There was famine in Ireland and dire poverty among the workers of town and countryside.

In March 1846 Derby's Liberal MPs both voted for the Tory Leader in the House of Commons, while both South Derbyshire Tory MPs voted against him! The Corn Laws were duly repealed and this was confirmed by the House of Lords in June. But on that bell-ringing Friday morning when the anti-Corn Laws people seemed to have influence in the parishes of St Alkmund and St Michael, Derbeians also heard that on the very same evening that he was successful in the Lords, Prime Minister Peel was beaten in the Commons and had to resign. Perhaps the Corn Law-wallers might have gone along with those bell-ringers after all!

The pendulum swung

For 40 years until his death in 1884, Derby was represented at Westminster by Liberal MP Michael Thomas Bass, plus one party colleague or another. Together with Joseph Strutt he was Derby's greatest Victorian benefactor. He represented the town when national politics was dominated by William Ewart Gladstone, four times Prime Minister, whom the Liberals were referring to as the G.O.M. ('Grand Old Man') by the end of the century. The Queen detested him and favoured his arch-rival and Conservative Leader, the charming Benjamin Disraeli. Gladstone was the object of endless criticism from the *Mercury*, always a Tory newspaper. In January 1897 the editor commented sarcastically on the report of the latest annual banquet the Derby Liberals had held on Mr Gladstone's birthday:

> Mr Gladstone is a great personality, and it is by no means an extraordinary thing that a company which 'numbered very few short of a hundred' should assemble in the Liberal Club to do honour to 'the Man that Was' [his prime ministerial days at last over]. For our part, we hope that Mr Gladstone may continue for many years to enjoy his physical and intellectual vigour – not only for his own sake, but that we may enjoy the pleasure of reading the speeches at the Derby Gladstone Banquet.

By then, however, the Tories' long wait for political power in Derby had ended. In the General Election of 1895 they won both of the town's parliamentary seats, which were now occupied by Sir Henry Bemrose and Sir Geoffrey Drage. The Party waited until the summer of 1897 to celebrate the victory in a 'Grand Demonstration' in Allestree Park, home of Sir William Gisborne. The *Mercury* claimed that their triumph in Derby had 'set the ball rolling [across the country] which resulted in the return of the Unionist [Conservative] Government by a great majority'. The July summer's day was fine and to the reporter the 'beautifully wooded park never looked more lovely'. From the time the park gates opened at one o'clock thousands streamed in towards the 'various marquees, band stands, &c.,' which had been 'erected on that large piece of ground which lies between the hall itself and the pretty pond on which so many people have disported themselves during the winter months' (presumably in skating, benefiting from the real winters of the 19th century!). There was a 'Parisian wizard' conjuror to gawp at, a 'grand assault-at-arms' by the Beaconsfield Athletics Club (Disraeli had been given the title Earl of Beaconsfield by his Queen), and dancing until the fete closed at 10 o'clock. For those not minded to enjoy 'a pleasant walk into Derby' along roads specially watered to keep down the dust that was a well-known drawback of Derbyshire routes at that time, 'cabs, brakes, and waggonettes were eagerly snatched up long before they reached the park gates'.

Allestree Hall, scene of the triumphant Conservative Party rally of 1897. (Photo: Dr Frank Jones)

There was a final political contest in Victorian times, known nationally as the Khaki Election, in the autumn of 1900. Derby Liberal Town Councillor Wilkins came under fierce attack in the *Mercury* of 5 September for speaking out at a meeting in Friar Gate Ward in support of a group in his party at Westminster who were against the Boer War. This had now been going on in South Africa for two years. Councillor Wilkins triggered an avalanche of angry letters to the editor, though, as he attempted to explain in a letter of his own, in his speech he had only set out to contrast the weak reasons for Britain going to war against the Boers with 'the enormous cost in valuable lives and some 70 millions of money that is being spent' (have we heard this sort of thing all over again recently?). A Borrowash scribe declared that 'I cannot think that my friend Mr Wilkins would side with such villainy, believing him to be a true Englishman and gentleman'.

There was an entirely new element about this election in Derby in the shape of a Labour candidate. Richard Bell, who earned his daily bread as the secretary of the union of 'Railway Servants', allied himself to the Liberals led by Sir Thomas Roe, a former Mayor of the town. The *Mercury* reported of Bell that 'meetings on his behalf are regularly held on Sunday mornings in Derby Market Place'. And of Sir Thomas, the editor claimed he 'has thrown

The commemorative plaque on the site of the Drill Hall recording an important aspect of the 1900 General Election result in Derby. (Photo: Dr Frank Jones)

himself unreservedly into the arms of Mr Bell, with his bundle of impracticable and socialistic dreams'. There was no doubting the *Mercury*'s position: 'we appeal to the electorate to support the achievement of the British Army. We who sit at home at ease have often enough regretted that we were not able more actively to support the British soldier. Now is your opportunity.'

Election day, 3 October, came round and the paper's reporter thought 'there was more blue [Tory] to be seen in the town than yellow [Liberal]'. The 'mural literature' included posters shouting 'Bemrose and Drage' on the one hand and 'Roe' and 'Bell' on the other. The Tories had the services of two motor cars. But surprise surprise, against the decisive national trend they were defeated, though narrowly, by majorities for Roe and Bell of 500 and 200 respectively out of nearly 30,000 votes registered in total. The *Daily News* called the Derby result the 'most remarkable' in the country. The electors of Derby had, equally remarkably, also chosen England's first-ever Labour MP, a fact commemorated now by a plaque on the wall of the Social Security Offices in Newland Street which stand on the site of the 1860s Drill Hall where the voting was done in 1900. The editor of the *Mercury* comforted himself with the reflection that the result 'will in no way be of more than local importance'. In Bell's case, little did he know!

For seats at Guildhall

In December 1856 the Tory *Mercury* had something to be cheerful about in local politics. Though, as the editor stated, ever since 'modern' town councils with elected Aldermen and Councillors had been set up by Act of Parliament in the 1830s Derby had been run by the

A misty Guildhall, every Mayor's kingdom, overlooking the outdoor market, horse-tram and statue of Thomas Bass in its original position, in profile to the Cornmarket, as placed in 1884 soon after his death. (Courtesy: Derby Museums and Art Gallery)

Liberal Party, in the most recent local election half-a-dozen Tories had won seats. This was a very good thing too for the *Mercury,* since it claimed that the Council had been far too 'liberal' with ratepayers' money. Sixteen thousand pounds had been added to the town debt. The editor moaned that his rival Liberal paper in town, *The Derby and Chesterfield Reporter,* thought that only Liberals were competent and intelligent enough to be councillors, indeed that 'Conservatives are not fit to live in this world, and there ought to be none existing; for they are not to be trusted either in public or private life'. This might now be proved wrong!

Of course, then as now there was plenty of moaning to be heard among the voters. Councillors came in for bashing, as in a letter to the *Mercury* in October 1878 signed simply 'An Elector':

> Sir – The annual farce of electing fit and proper persons to serve the ratepayers and the town generally being near at hand it may not be out of place to make a few practical remarks, gathered from a bird's-eye experience of the past. The chief qualification required for candidates in the present day appears to be anything in the shape of a man with two legs who can talk; brains are a secondary consideration. An educated jackdaw or magpie might answer the same purposes only for appearances.

There was no attempt here to disguise contempt! Neither was the Mayor spared, as in a letter signed 'Civis' in October 1897:

> Sir – It is high time that the citizens of Derby showed that they thought it a matter of moment who should be chief magistrate of this large and important borough. We have had some most excellent Mayors, and also some quite unfitted to occupy the position, and it is more by good luck than good management that no important emergency has arisen to show their incapacity. Yet at Mayor's dinners and other public occasions the same fulsome flattery has been ladled out with strict impartiality on men of energy and ability and the amiable duffers who have struggled through their year of office without doing any particular harm. I am not referring to spending large sums of money. That has often been quoted by friends of candidates as if it were the sole qualification, and they have stated in round figures how many thousands their man was going to spend if elected. These thousands have never been spent, and I am glad of it, for I don't think the honour should be bought. We have to bewail the extreme difficulty of persuading suitable men to join the Corporation, and is not this trouble likely to increase if elevation to the chair is understood to be merely a matter of patient waiting?'

Problems, challenges and endorsements

Councillors had plenty on their plate in Victorian times too. There were relatively simple, low-level problems that with human nature being what it was could take a long time to solve and kept coming round again. So Mayor W. Eaton Mousley in November 1846 vowed in the Guildhall not to 'relax in his endeavours to put down the broils in low public houses – to abolish Sunday trading, which he abhorred – and to abate the brutal play of foot-ball'. The last on this list did come to an end. It wasn't the same game at which the Rams were to achieve distinction at the Baseball Ground much later in the century, but the mass-participation variety that still somehow thrives in Ashbourne a century and a half later and caused mayhem and discomfort to indifferent pedestrians on Derby streets until it was indeed put a stop to.

Then there were the bigger issues and challenges, such as the will to put through the painful changes necessary to adapt a basically mediaeval pattern of streets to the demands of a time of greater mobility and expanding industry. This sort of thing was of course in addition to a whole range of problems close to home such as housing, drainage and waste disposal that might be termed the 'bread and butter' of councillors' responsibilities. Between 1860 and 1880 a massive programme of widening old thoroughfares like Queen Street, Iron Gate, St Peter's Street and the Wardwick and of adding new ones like St James's Street, Becket Street and the Strand was carried through, to be followed by the laying down of the tram routes.

From 1867 to 1877 the Council took on another sort of challenge, to expand the boundaries of the Borough and so its own authority to include the smaller neighbours of Litchurch and Little Chester. Litchurch was between a third and a half of the size of Derby Borough at that

Looking down St Peter's Street in about 1873 after demolition for widening had begun. The Nag's Head pub on the right has already gone. (Courtesy: Derby Museums and Art Gallery)

time. The spur for this campaign for expansion was the substantial increase in the number of voters in the Borough as a consequence of the Second Reform Bill passed through Parliament by Disraeli's Conservative Government. The parliamentary constituencies, the areas within which voters chose an MP to represent them, had to be altered and it made sense, at least to a majority of Derby Borough councillors, to take in Litchurch so that reasonably sized areas could be created for this purpose. However, a majority of the people of Litchurch thought otherwise. They had an ally on the Borough Council in the person of Alderman Roe, who must have voiced one of their main thoughts on the issue, at a time when Iron Gate must have looked not much better than a demolition site in the middle of being widened and the splendid new Market Hall had been completed just the previous year, when he accused fellow councillors of wanting to make Litchurch folk 'pay for the improvements that had been made in the borough'. On the other hand, Alderman Madeley responded that with a population getting on for 11,000 and the disgraceful 'rows, drunken fights, and brawls that frequently took place' there, 'a source of great annoyance to the peaceable inhabitants', Litchurch was ripe for a takeover. Lots of people who lived there found employment in the Borough, some streets had one side in Derby and the other in Litchurch and 'an immense amount of heavy traffic' passed to and fro between the one and the other. He carried the day: councillors voted 17 to 14 in favour of incorporation, perhaps not a convincing majority, in September 1867.

At any rate, the representatives of the people of Litchurch turned up to their meeting-room in Bloomfield Place the next week and emphatically turned down the proposal from across their border. The Boundary Commissioners from London who had to decide on the issue then called a public meeting in October at the St Andrew's Schoolroom, advertised by means of hand-bills. Getting on for 140 people turned up and by 90 to five backed their representatives' decision. One man was reported making what must have been a key statement on this occasion, that many would have been in favour of being represented at Westminster in this way 'had it not been the case that if they joined the borough and had a vote, they would have to pay what they did not already pay, a rate (Hear, hear)'. When it came to Darley Abbey's turn, also included in the takeover plan, the owner of Darley Hall Mr Henry Evans handled the affair in true paternal style and, armed with a sheet of signatures, said that 'every inhabitant desired not to be annexed to the borough of Derby'. Ten years later this exact fate did befall Litchurch and Little Chester but it took another century for the successors of the monks to change their minds.

Going for space

An issue that kept coming up time and again, especially after 1870, was the expansion of parks in Derby. Joseph Strutt's generosity in giving to the town his 11-acre private grounds just beyond the Union Workhouse off the Osmaston Road, after having it redesigned as an arboretum by the foremost garden designer of the day, John Claudius Loudon, meant that from September 1840 Derby had become the proud possessor of the very first publicly-run park in Britain. Its donor had been remarkably quick off the mark in responding to the Liberal Parliament's plea for health-giving open spaces for the new masses of millworkers cooped up in manufacturing towns and cities at a time when railways were in their infancy and excursions to far-off places were not so cheap. So Derby's Arboretum became the favoured

Statue of Joseph Strutt over the main entrance to the Arboretum, the work of John Loudon and Henry Duesbury in 1853, 10 years after the donor's death. (Photo: Andrew Butterton)

destination of some of the first day-excursions by the new-fangled rail from Nottingham, Leicester, Sheffield and Birmingham. This was especially so when it was decided to repeat annually on Strutt's birthday in July (he died in 1843) the kind of celebrations that took place at its opening. These were quite something, with circus-type acts and especially balloon ascents, which were kept up when the festival was pushed back into June in the 1850s.

In July 1846 the *Mercury* reported that 'we believe we are not exaggerating when we state that upwards of five thousand people came in special trains alone'. Total attendance was a record 15,000, with takings of £200. By then the park had been enhanced with the addition of a fountain to add to the other ornaments (in particular the so-called and much-loved 'Florentine Boar' on its pedestal), vases and urns that Joseph Strutt had transferred from his private gardens. The previous year a field adjoining the park at its south-eastern corner and at a right-angle to it, suitable for sports including football, had been bought by the Council and enhanced by avenues of trees on its longer sides ending in Rosehill Street. At its far end along that street a glass structure that became known locally as 'The Crystal Palace', rather similar in appearance to the giant that would be put up in Hyde Park in London six years later, was paid for by subscribers led by the Duke of Devonshire and to be used for refreshments and other ancillary activities. It was the backdrop in 1888 to a famous victory by Derby Junction football team over mighty Blackburn Rovers in the quarter-finals of the FA Cup! Finally in 1853 the Arboretum was provided with a grand new entrance presided over by a statue of Strutt in the attitude of an Ancient Roman.

Despite the entertainments, the brass, military and quadrille bands, the performing dogs, the 'Continental Gymnasts', comedians, dancers and above all the balloon ascents by such as Emmanuel Jackson, so-called 'Midlands Astronaut', there were criticisms of how the Arboretum was run. It wasn't free, except on Sundays and Wednesdays, until the 1880s, so in this respect Derby was soon overtaken by new parks in other towns and cities like Nottingham. It didn't appear to have been adequately cared for, so that in February 1878 Councillor Leech could say this of it: 'The condition of things had so changed that the plants which were to afford botanical study had died, and smoke had come all around the place, and the delicate plants which died were not replaced. Therefore the place had become simply a place of recreation.' The editor of the *Mercury* added that 'with the iron-foundries and pottery

The 'Florentine Boar', a recent replica of the copy of an Italian work of 1805 seen by Joseph Strutt on holiday and brought to his home at Thorntree House and later transferred to the Arboretum to accompany his gift to the town. The original was badly damaged during a World War Two air raid. (Photo: Andrew Butterton)

kilns sending forth their fumes' the trees would soon be 'transformed into rows of blackened skeletons'. In addition, 'Mr Giles, another working man, characterised the "crystal palace" as a "disgrace" in its present condition'. There was even criticism as early as June 1846 of the way the anniversary celebrations themselves were run. The *Mercury* published a letter signed 'One of the Uncomfortable Ladies' complaining about the organisers doing away with a special enclosure 'where the most respectable portion of the visitors used to congregate to witness the filling of the balloon' and which provided 'a retreat from the annoyance of the universal cigar smoking'. The good lady maintained that the authorities were also throwing away good money doing away with this enclosure because 'hundreds of people would most willingly have paid their sixpences for the privilege of seeing, for instance, such an exhibition as that of the clever dogs, whose heads were now and then tantalizingly visible over the heads of some four or five thousand of the most able-bodied *pushers*'. The writer concluded by telling the editor that 'I overheard ladies declare, that "unless something of the sort was done, they should be unable to attend the *fete* next year".'

Indeed, by April 1878 the Arboretum itself was in dire trouble. Instead of being right at the southern edge of the town, as it had been when a family retreat of the Strutts, it was now surrounded by terraced houses and other buildings. The new suburb of Rosehill was where many of the Midland Railway's employees lived and the enclosed area of the Arboretum, still not free to access, meant quite a detour for them to and from their work around the station. Consequently Alderman Leech on the Council proposed driving a road through the park to 'get around' this difficulty. The proposal was approved at a meeting of Arboretum Ward ratepayers and noted by the Council. It was backed by the *Mercury* editor, who proclaimed the Park was a nuisance, a barrier to proper lines of communication:

> Temple Bar did the same in London, but that obstruction has been removed. The Arboretum is quite as much out of place in a growing manufacturing district as the other anachronism was in the heart of a populous city. Why not sell the land and lay out streets which may satisfy the requirements of the population? An Act of Parliament applied for by the Corporation would, we suppose, be easily obtained, giving power to deal with the property; and the money got from the sale thereof for building purposes, might be laid out in the purchase of a public park elsewhere. Osmaston Park at one end of the town and Markeaton Park at the other may not, in process of time, be wholly unattainable.

We may applaud the editor's crystal ball-gazing, but surely not his downgrading of an historic gift to the status of mere 'property'!

However, at a further meeting, this time of Litchurch ratepayers, at the end of February 1878 Alderman Leech's scheme was overturned and a footpath substituted, soon to be made possible when admission charges to the Arboretum were abolished for good. The *Mercury*'s editor was miffed. It was obviously an extremely lively, if not downright raucous meeting, summarised by the paper as a 'Screaming Farce'. A difference of opinion about 'cutting up the Arboretum' was perfectly in order, 'but there can be no question whatever about the worse-than-uselessness of such exhibitions of buffoonery as did duty for discussion' and 'to call the

One of the vases that graced the gift of the Arboretum and the rear of the main entrance, recently restored. (Photo: Andrew Butterton)

decision of such a meeting an expression of public opinion would be an insult to common sense'. A letter came to the editor signed by 'Three Large Ratepayers' claiming that their like actually voted for Alderman Leech's proposal whereas the opposition who won the day:

> ... comprised of a large number of lads in their teens, and a considerable amount of the residuum of the low public-houses of the neighbourhood who had evidently been collected together, and having been duly refreshed, were ready for any work their employers dictated. We name those facts to show how utterly worthless is the opinion of a public meeting which is packed to obtain a foregone conclusion.

Is democracy compromised by hard work behind the scenes?

Over 10 years earlier in June 1867 the Arboretum had been joined as a place of recreation by another open space at the northern edge of the Midland Railway complex itself, again as a result of the generosity of an individual. The Bass Recreation Ground between the River Derwent and the mill flume or outlet channel for the mills in the area known as the Morledge was presented to the town by its longest serving MP, who would, 11 years later, as we have already seen, present it with its Free Library. Though its three acres was only just over a quarter of the size of the Arboretum, it became a much treasured green space, easily large enough, according to the *Mercury* report, to contain the 8–10,000 Derbeians who turned up to celebrate its Saturday afternoon opening. Its object was made clear by Thomas Bass himself in his reply to the Mayor's words of praise on behalf of the Corporation: 'I have been young and am now old, but I never can forget the days of my youth; and I very frequently reflect on the advantages of play and recreation. "Too much work makes Jack a dull boy".'

Bass Recreation Ground, Thomas Bass's first major gift to the town he represented in Parliament for 35 years, opened in 1867. (Photo: Dr Frank Jones)

So now there was a park towards the southern end of town and one near the centre. In January 1878 there was a clamour for one for north Derby. The Guildhall was full of mostly 'working men' on a Thursday evening for the start of the campaign. The Mayor gave them to understand that good Mr Bass had offered £1,000 towards the target. Mr Ward urged speedy action because suitable land 'was being continually absorbed for building purposes, and although they might even now have to go a little further out for the land than would appear desirable, yet in 10 years time it would be comparatively near'. He pointed to the need in referring to 'the mischief into which children were likely to get when they played in the streets, and stated the difficulty he found to censure lads who ventured to trespass in a field he occupied on the Ashbourne Road'. A Mr Walton thought it was 'all very well for those who could go away from the town at certain seasons of the year and enjoy themselves; these no doubt could content themselves with the town the rest of the year with a nice place to live in, but those who had not these advantages wanted this place of recreation'.

Two areas focussed attention. There was Strutt's Park off Duffield Road up for sale by Lord Belper. In May the *Mercury* printed a letter by someone describing him/herself as 'a large ratepayer' who thought Lord Belper was asking far too much for his 60 acres. Though he praised its 'sublime landscape in this beautiful month of May', its owner was asking twice as much per acre as it cost speculators to acquire the Firs Estate 12 months earlier. Strutt's Park was 'a very pleasant walk around the outside, and if it is ever cut up for building purposes [it was indeed!] there will be plenty of promenades for health and recreation'. A much better bet he/she thought would be Rowditch, which the Corporation already owned. It was easy to get to with the brand new Great Northern Railway line running on one side of it. In fact this was the next park to materialise, but it still took another 10 years to arrive. The crucial meeting, after two councillors managed to stop in the nick of time the six-and-a-half acres, including an 'old disused militia barracks and drill ground on the Old Uttoxeter Road', from being sold for building, took place at the Guildhall on a Friday evening in early April 1888. The Rowditch ground was described as being within easy access of the parishes of St Barnabas on one side and St Luke's on the other, both areas of frantic expansion. The *Mercury* editor concluded:

> The open spaces which are left are rapidly being built upon, and the only playground in a vast number of cases is the street. No wonder the Mayor feels, as he told the meeting on Friday night, the magisterial duty that he likes the least is fining boys for playing football in the streets. The present is an opportunity which will never occur again, for no open space so central and so suitable in every way is left.

Derwent Bank, target of park campaigners for north Derby in 1897. It was not to be acquired by the Council till many years later. (Photo: Andrew Butterton)

The rumblings in favour of something in the true north of town continued but by October 1897 when another despairing correspondent appealed in the *Mercury* for a new benefactor to come to the rescue, Bass had now been missed for 13 years; only the grounds of Derwent Bank, former home of Thomas Bridgett, who built Rykneld Mills back in 1821, was left of the Strutt Park estate and were now up for sale too. The writer declared that 'there is no town I know of so badly off as regards public parks as Derby' – a mournful reflection on developments since 1840 surely! It compared unfavourably with neighbouring Burton 'with its Worthington's Recreation Ground and Trent Side Park'. But it made no difference. Additional open green space had to await the 20th century, with the exception of a few acres between the Kedleston and Ashbourne Roads donated by 'Mr Mundy' of Markeaton Hall and which was added to in the 1900s by his widow. Some ratepayers thought Bass and his like a menace, indeed 'an unmitigated curse' for the town. This was a sentiment expressed in a letter to the *Mercury* in October 1878 signed 'A Native' who confessed that:

I was resting under the hopeful impression that the scheme to provide a public park at the expense of the ratepayers had been consigned to the shades of oblivion. If it is the intention of our local rulers to try experiments of visionary madness by pampering with luxury the sons and daughters of idleness and improvidence out of the hard earnings and striving of others, there is an end to thrift, and no encouragement to provide for a rainy day. Those who have private property in the borough may as well hand over the title deeds at once to the Town Clerk, and save the future annoyance of being filched of it by successive instalments, until the whole has vanished into the air castle region of folly and waste.

Triumph

One of the occasional functions of the Mayor in particular as chief citizen of the town as well as leader of the Council was to take a lead in organising the celebration of very special events in the life of the country. There were at least three of these in the long span of Victoria's reign.

Florence Nightingale, commemorated as 'The Lady of the Lamp' on and off the London Road near the DRI. (Photos: Andrew Butterton)

In May 1856 Derby, like every other town in the country, felt called upon to rejoice on the conclusion of peace after the two long years of the Crimean War in far-off Russia. Over 30 years later there was the Golden Jubilee of 1887, followed 10 years later in June 1897 by the celebration of the Great Queen's Diamond Jubilee.

Though the Derbyshire Regiment played a distinguished part in the fighting and Florence Nightingale of Lea Hurst near Cromford won undying fame in the Crimea, it was all very far away indeed, on the easternmost borders of Europe. In early April 1856, when the war was nearly over, the *Mercury's* editor commented on the lack of enthusiasm being shown, presumably in Derby, at the news of celebrations in Paris and London for the declaration of peace. People didn't yet 'know what it is they have to be joyful for'. They 'have yet scarcely felt the pressure of the war; they have not been forced to alter their usual style of living, or to forgo any of their luxuries. They have had heavy taxes to pay, it is true. Only by the loss of relatives and friends and by the former sufferings of our army have we been made painfully aware that we have, for the last two years, been waging war with one of the great European powers.' In January, though, the paper had pointed out that those who lived in the meaner streets of the borough were experiencing privations. As always, war had meant higher prices, hitting the poor the hardest. And the actual battles in the Crimea would certainly influence the Council when it came to naming new residential streets when the war was over – Alma, Cardigan, Nightingale, Raglan.

However, at the end of April the Mayor, after sending out circulars, chaired a meeting in the Guildhall of a hundred 'clergy, gentry and principal inhabitants of the town' to decide how best to celebrate 'the restoration of peace'. He noted in his speech that there were some people who actually wanted hostilities to continue (because they thought the Russians had got off far too lightly) but he made his own feelings perfectly clear: 'considering the amount of privations, sufferings, death, ever inseparable from war, I am at a loss to understand how any really thoughtful and humane person can do otherwise than rejoice that the sword has been restored to its scabbard (Hear, hear)'. In fact the editor of the *Mercury* himself was unhappy with the terms of the peace because he appeared to have an immense fear of Russia, contrasting with his very favourable attitude to the United States.

The great day, Wednesday 21 May, arrived:

> As early as four o'clock in the morning cannons and guns were discharged from various places in the town – a feature in the celebration which was continued during the day; to these succeeded pistols and crackers, the juveniles wakening the elderlies sooner than their wont; afterwards the bells of the five parish churches rang out their merry peals, and by nine o'clock the appearance of the streets testified that the people had determined to keep high holiday.

There were flags and banners, evergreens and 'floral wreathes' in every street. Special trains brought in thousands and many others came in from the surrounding villages. A gigantic mile-and-a-half-long procession of 'Sunday scholars', members of Friendly Societies and Iron Foundry workers from Litchurch, in front of a 'triumphal car' carrying Derby's Crimean heroes, each with a laurel wreath on his head, passed before the Town

Celebrating the coming of
peace in 1856 at the corner of
Market Head and Rotten
Row. (Courtesy: Derby
Museums and Art Gallery)

Hall. Messrs Keene and Bemrose published the work of photographers among the crowd. Of their results the *Mercury* commented: 'Those representing the procession are indistinct; the buildings, with flags suspended from them, are, however, delineated with perfect fidelity'. An ox 'roasted in the open space between the lower end of Full Street and the Derwent' was cut up and given with 'several round of beef' to 700 poor people. One hundred enjoyed roast sheep for 1s at the Temperance Hall and sheep were also roasted at a whole host of pubs. Manufacturing and other firms dined their workers, though sadly only some of the larger ones included wives if the *Mercury* report was indeed accurate. One firm, Messrs Bridgett & Co. of Rykneld Mills, took their weavers off to Birmingham, with the band of the 1st Derby Militia leading them to the station, 'to visit some of the wonders of the manufacturing metropolis'. Of course, much of all this activity was privately organised, adding to the core official event.

There was in fact another minor bout of war celebration 45 years later in May 1900. This time the fighting was even further away in an entirely different direction. It was the middle of the Boer War in South Africa which had provided a shock for the British when the mighty Queen's forces found themselves locked up in two towns, Ladysmith and Mafeking. When they finally managed to get out there was maniacal rejoicing. It was quite strong in March when the news came that the siege of Ladysmith had been broken. The *Mercury* office at the bottom of Iron Gate had put out a Union Flag at 10 o'clock in the morning when the printing machines had started into action on receipt of the information, with the result that 'the passers-by promptly grasping its import raised a cheer'. Soon the newsboys were shouting it all about the town and anyone who had a flag flew it out of the window! Ladies dressed in the national colours, dogs were similarly decorated and 'little boys waved coloured handkerchiefs in their joy'. Bells rang out and bunting followed over the streets.

But that was nothing compared to the scene in May when Mafeking was relieved, Robert Baden-Powell and all. The *Mercury* waxed lyrical:

> Derby's patriotism does not often take the form of popular demonstration, but Saturday night was an exception to the rule, and the main streets of the usually undemonstrative town were converted into a veritable pandemonium by the blowing of innumerable horns and the singing and cheering of a crowd of young men, who noisily paraded the streets. In all the churches and chapels yesterday references were made to the brave defenders of that far-away outpost of the Empire, and in almost every case the National Anthem was fervently sung by the congregation.

On the Thursday of the following week, also the Queen's birthday, the Council weighed in with the official celebrations. The town was

Rykneld Mills, the largest textile manufactory in early Victorian times, whose owners treated their employees to a Jubilee outing in 1897. (Photo: Andrew Butterton)

Were these Iron Gate promenaders celebrating the relief of Ladysmith, or Mafeking, in far away South Africa in 1900? (Courtesy: Derby Museums and Art Gallery)

Derby man in full fighting kit for the South African (Boer) War 1899–1902.
(Courtesy: W.W. Winter)

once again 'awash with flags', factory workers were given the day off, effigies of Kruger the Boer leader and his wife were burnt, there was an official service in the Guildhall, a procession behind a band, more bands and crowds in the Arboretum and all recreation grounds in the afternoon, sheep-roasting in Wood's Lane in the evening, a firework display until 10pm on Chester Green and 'monster bonfires on Bass's Recreation Ground, at Rowditch and on Dale Road Estate'.

By then, however, the Jack and Jill of all celebrations had happened three Junes previously in 1897!

Jubilee...

It was 60 years since Victoria had first entered Buckingham Palace and every community in the country wanted to do something about it. For example, out in Derbyshire Quarndon resolved to put a clock on the church tower, Alfreton to build public baths and Ashbourne a cottage hospital, Findern to plant a 'Jubilee Tree' on the village green and Mickleover to put a drinking trough and pump in the village square. In the county town a Celebration Fund of well over £1,000 was directed by a sub-committee to illuminate the Guildhall with 'electric glow lamps'. A beacon was to shine from the Shot Tower in the Morledge, there were 'monster bonfires' on Bass's Recreation Ground again, at the top of Nottingham Road by the entrance to the cemetery, on Markeaton and Rowditch Recreation Grounds, and in Pear Tree near Randolph Street and by the Pear Tree Station. When the great day arrived, Sunday 20 June, the main event was a Civic Service at All Saints'. The Mayor, Sir Thomas Roe, and his Councillors were escorted by a party of no fewer than 400 troops from Normanton Barracks, who walked through densely packed streets, wet from heavy rain in the night and still falling slightly under leaden skies and bedraggled bunting. Bands led and brought up the rear of the procession. The Bishop of Derby preached an appropriate sermon and after the service was over came 'the joyous clanging of the bells of All Saints'.' On the Monday evening the Mayor presided over a banquet for the Aldermen, Councillors, Magistrates and 'many other prominent citizens' at the Albert Hall of the Mechanics Institution in the Wardwick.

That Monday also saw crowds of people in town to see the illuminations and decorations, especially in the Market Place. Next day was the official Jubilee holiday and was blessed with

The Guildhall presiding over the Market Place, always the focus of municipal celebrations as in the Jubilee of 1897. (Courtesy: Derby Local Studies Library)

proverbial 'Queen's weather', the sun shining from early morning on. Many people wore patriotic colours and the trams were similarly decorated. In the Market Place the over 3,000 electric lamps festooning the Town Hall created a 'magnificent' impression, and 'on all hands it was agreed that the sight was by far the grandest of its kind ever seen in Derby'. People on King Street walked under a garland with a flag in the centre near the Old Flower Pot and Derby School (St Helen's House) was 'covered with flags and shields and bunting'. On Chester Green no fewer than six thousand children sang the National Anthem in the afternoon in the presence of the Mayor and they followed it with three cheers for the Queen. There were assemblies of children too at the other recreation grounds. In the evening, besides the bonfires, rockets were fired from the Shot Tower. A party of 30 to 40 Derbeians also decided to swell the most prominent county bonfire party, high up on the top of 900ft Crich Hill. They were rewarded with a 'panoramic view of beacons on neighbouring and far-distant peaks'. The one on Kinder could be picked out, as could Longstone Edge, Masson, Bessyloan, Chevin and even the Shot Tower itself back down the valley. According to the *Mercury*, 'no less than the astonishing number of 81 beacons could be counted with the naked eye!' Indeed:

> …some of those from Derby lingered long on the summit watching the beacons dying away, and though the broadening glow in the eastern sky beckoned the break of dawn before they arrived back in Derby, they felt that they had been privileged spectators of an historic display such as this or any other country has never before witnessed.

... and disaster

A little over a fortnight later, on a July summer evening, the Jubilee rejoicing must have been blanked out in the consciousness of both Derby's chief citizen and many of his poorer fellow townspeople. The Borough Fire Brigade, one of the main services for which he was responsible, was unable to save the very foundation of Sir Thomas Roe's standing in the town as well as the houses of well over a hundred poor people. A devastating fire broke out just before a quarter to seven in the Roe family sawmills and timber yard off Siddals Road, next to Sir John Smith and Son's foundry and cheek-by-jowl with courts, tenements and narrow terraced streets. The sawmills were one of the largest in the Midlands, employing 130 workmen. Even though the firemen got there in one minute and a half, enormous damage was done, so fierce was the blaze, and up to 20 houses and between 60 and 80 tenements suffered more or less serious torching.

Sir Thomas wasn't even in town. He learnt of the disaster by telegram on reaching St Pancras Station after leaving a Council meeting and catching the 5.30pm train for London. It was 'probably the most serious conflagration which has occurred in Derby within the memory of its oldest inhabitant', according to the *Mercury*. It 'undoubtedly originated in a shed in the vicinity of the boilers and chimney in the northern corner of the works'. Fanned by a breeze, it had got to the huge stack of timber in the yard by the time the firemen arrived. The sufferings of the nearby householders were compounded by the apparently suspect energy of many of those who descended on the area ostensibly to help! 'Household goods – tons of them – were thrown through the windows pell mell into the street, which resulted in the destruction of an enormous amount of furniture'.

The Rural Dean of Derby set up a relief centre in St Andrew's Schools nearby and on the morning after the blaze nearly a hundred people were able gratefully to eat an early breakfast at Trinity Church Mission Hall. After expressing deep sympathy with Sir Thomas the Council opened a subscription list to help his unfortunate fellow sufferers. Alderman Marsden, in enthusiastically backing this move, reported that 'no less than 60 houses had been wrecked by mis-directed and sympathising friends'. They removed everything 'including £20 from the yard foreman's house' and he had 'heard of one poor woman whose sewing machine had been stolen but he hoped that the article would be returned'. The *Mercury*'s regular 'Local Echoes' column enlarged upon this sort of thing:

> Let a house stand empty a little while, and unless it is closely watched someone is sure to get in. There is a story that even in Hartington Street [a very respectable gated locality built nearly 20 years earlier with Woodiwiss family money] once upon a time an uninhabited house was cleared of its marble mantelpieces, grates, and bell wires; and the height of impudence was reached in another place where a new wall had been partly knocked down, and the owner discovered a man with a horse and cart removing the bricks. The man objected to remonstrances, and with an air of injured innocence protested that he was only 'shifting the rummel'. It is exceedingly difficult to keep empty property from becoming dilapidated, and thieving at fires always takes place.

However, by the following week nearly £600 had been subscribed for those who had lost out in the fire and nearly all of the Siddals Road workmen had been taken on at 'branch establishments'.

Despite the fire brigade's best efforts the blaze provided a memorable spectacle to the hundreds of Derbeians who either responded to 'the headlong career of the borough engine from the town' or the rumours 'that something untoward was happening', or spotted the 'great column of brown smoke which rose up from the burning timber yard immediately on the outbreak of the flames'. People on the west side of Derby on that otherwise beautiful evening couldn't see the flames because of the taller buildings in the town centre, but a *Mercury* letter-writer from Dalbury Lees stated that 'the smoke of the great fire on Wednesday night was noticed by persons not only in that village but as far out as Long Lane and Thurvaston'. The best view of things was from the Nottingham Road bridge over the Derwent and there 'a small crowd of spectators assembled, noting the occasional leaps of flames – 50 or 60 feet high perhaps – and the play of the water jets sparkling in the sunshine'.

The Mayor would surely never forget that July evening in 1897! Just as K. Keys, writing in *Ward and Co.'s Annual* for 1892, could not forget a disaster from quite the opposite cause back on April Fool's Day 1842 when, after torrential rain, the centre of town was swamped by the Markeaton Brook to a depth commemorated by a plaque in the Wardwick. He wrote:

Flood marker opposite the Mechanics' Institution commemorating the height in the Wardwick of the great flood on April Fools' Day 1842. (Photo: Andrew Butterton)

I was living with my parents in Willow Row at the time. I remember watching the water surging down the street, when a rather eccentric cow-keeper, named Dudley, who lived in an adjoining court ... passed by, mounted on the back of one of his cows, and driving the others in front ... on his head was a night-cap ... As he approached Sadler Gate Bridge the current was so strong that had it not been for Mr Horsley's (a bookbinder) presence of mind in letting down a sheet for him to cling to, the comedy would have ended in a tragedy. He pulled himself up into Mr Horsley's house, while the cows ascended the bridge, and stayed there till the waters subsided.

It was another reminder of how close county town and country were in Victorian days.

CHAPTER 9

Time Off

BOROUGH OF DERBY, FISHING IN THE RIVER DERWENT. The Mayor and Magistrates have been informed that Poaching, by the setting of night lines, and unfair angling, by one person using several rods and lines at one time, have been practised in that part of the River Derwent within the boundaries of the Borough; and whereas such mal-practices are injurious to the fair angler,

IT IS HEREBY ORDERED, That no angler in the said Borough waters shall use more than one rod and line at one time, and that no fishing whatever be permitted before sunrise, nor later than one hour after sunset, and the Police and the River-watchers have instructions to take notice of all persons acting in violation of these orders, in order that they may be proceeded against according to law. ROBERT PELL, Mayor, September 2nd, 1856.

(*Derby Mercury*, 3 September 1856)

So the guardians of the Law took issue with at least one leisure activity. Izaak Walton's *Compleat Angler* had his followers 200 years after his creator's death, though the people targeted by the Mayor here would probably be gazing into far murkier waters than the crystal Dove the prince of anglers was used to. The Derwent was at least wider at Derby and as we have seen its eastern bank would have been far less enclosed by building in earlier Victorian days than it is today. But it must have been getting more and more polluted as the 19th century passed by, since the town's modern sewage system was not opened until the early years of the 20th century. The *Mercury*'s fishing correspondent, George Eaton, lived many miles upstream at Starkholmes near Matlock and his favourite waters were farther up still, beyond the junction with the Wye at Rowsley. Chatsworth Park was a favoured playground, which those able to afford transport from the county town might well have accessed too.

There was then less surface squeamishness about the taking of life. In June 1867 Mr Eaton advised: 'A man to get anything like a dish of fish must wade, working as much up stream and across under the opposite bank as possible'. In December: 'I had a day on the Chatsworth length on Thursday. There are plenty of fish, but they require fine and careful fishing to kill them.' There may have been a price to pay, all too familiar to us now. That September a correspondent signing himself 'GILDEROY' had complained:

> … having fished these rivers for the last 20 years, I can unhesitatingly assert that, although there is no lack of fish, still for several years there has been a marked falling off in the sport, attributable, in my humble opinion, to the merciless way in which the waters are flogged. The fact is that the fish are never allowed to rest, and perhaps there is scarcely a yard of the rivers that is not fished over once or oftener every day. The Wye, one of the finest grayling streams in the Midland Counties, is ruined by the indiscriminate issue of day-tickets, instead of the permission being restricted (as it ought to be) to the persons staying at the hotels at either end of the water.

Obviously a democrat here! But the pleasure continued of course. In May 1888 the *Mercury* reprinted a piece from the *London Standard* that must have stirred the nostrils of the average Derby angler:

> Fishing in Derbyshire is everywhere gratifying just now. All along the Dove the local flies are killing well, for the breeze — and it was boisterous indeed last week — has settled, and the weather is delightful. Nice dishes of trout have appeared on the tables of the Izaak Walton and the Peveril, and rodsters who know the water right away from the bend near Thorpe Cloud up to the Fishing House never remember the river better stocked. The olive dun, the whirling blue, and the March brown have been favourite flies, and in the more secluded parts of Miller's Dale have been very effective.

And what an agreeable reminder of the glories on Derby's doorstep!

The hunters

The more instantly recognisable blood-sport of fox-hunting would no doubt have directly affected very few Derbeians. It was the concern of the gentry and minor aristocracy of the country round about. To the north lay the lair of the Meynell hounds, to the south those of the Earl of Harrington. Since the Meynells met on the Monday, Thursday and Saturday of each week the concept of 'time off' or leisure must have been rather blurred at the edges when applied to the hunt! In November 1888 the Meynell made a move into town, which obviously involved the cream of Derby society when the Hunt met on a Thursday morning at Park Fields, Kedleston Road, 'the residence of Mr G. Wheeldon'. George Wheeldon, Mayor in 1873, had made his money as a maltster. Mixing that day with the likes of the Earl of Harrington of Elvaston and one of the Curzons of Kedleston Hall were, in addition to the host, Capt. Wheeldon and Mr A.S. Haslam (of another of the town's industrial dynasties). Despite it being 'dull and threatening' there were according to the *Mercury* 'a large number of spectators' to see the hounds off at 11.30 'in the direction of Darley osier beds'.

The hunts impinged on the town more in a social sense, at least as a spectacle, in the form of the annual Hunt Ball at the Assembly Rooms. One of the events of the year, this occasion helped to maintain the image of Derby as a county town, which by mid-Victorian times would no longer have been reinforced by the presence of town houses where county families had formerly spent the winter. Before 1850 the Assembly Rooms were usually given the prefix 'New' in *Mercury* reports, though Derby architect Joseph Pickford's splendid work was now over half a century old. In January 1837 the Hunt Ball there was 'most fashionably attended. The supper consisted of every delicacy in season, and was admirably served up, reflecting great credit on the taste and management of Mrs and the Misses Wallis [of the King's Head Hotel in the Corn-market].' In November 1838, when advertising that season's version for the following month, the *Mercury* added that 'We understand that the Marquess of Hastings, and Mr Meynell's Hounds will hunt in the immediate neighbourhood during that week'. There was a more fulsome report in December 1846: the Ball 'on the night of Wednesday last' was:

> … one of the most spirited and numerously attended assemblies that has taken place for many years past. The hall was opened at 10 o'clock, and dancing commenced to the delightful strains of a band specially engaged for the occasion from London. One hundred and eighty-nine members of the leading families in the county were present, and dancing was continued at intervals with unabated spirit until half-past 4 o'clock in the morning.

The tradition continued, though by January 1878 it was perhaps playing second social fiddle to the County (New Year) Ball on the first Wednesday evening of the year. In February 1897 the *Mercury* announced: 'LORD SCARSDALE will entertain a large house party this week at Kedleston Hall, for the Meynell Hunt Ball, which is to take place at Derby this (Wednesday) night'.

Horses for courses

Where the ordinary citizen of Derby might have been able to breathe the same air, if not quite fill the same enclosure, but definitely enjoy the same sporting thrill as the gentle families from the fine houses on the town's edge, was the racecourse. The prospect of the Derby races had, as we have seen, reduced numbers for the Lincoln rail excursion in September 1846. It was a much looked forward to calendar event. In May 1838 the horses raced over 'two large meadows in the possession of Mr Collinson, at Litchurch, a short distance from Derby. The opinion was general that the course surpassed the old one in the Siddals, being much more circular, and without the two dangerous sharp turns, so generally complained of by the jockeys.' However, in October 1846 they were back in the Siddals, though it would not be for long before the races would move a little further out as the adjacent Midland Railway complex continued to expand. Punters could see a new grandstand under construction on the far side of the river. Meanwhile, over two days, a Tuesday and Wednesday, special railway excursions would feed the old site, and 'booths, &c., will be erected in the field adjoining the course'. The occasion would have wider importance in the world of sport according to the *Mercury*: 'Handsome subscriptions have been given by noblemen and gentlemen of the town and county, and we are informed that a large party of the elite of the sporting world will assemble at Bretby Hall [the noble Earl of Chesterfield's family home], and patronize the races. Gaming booths and tables will be prohibited.' In the event the crowd, on a fine afternoon following a wet morning that made the ground 'anything but pleasant or suitable for pedestrians', must have been decidedly low-class in composition. While there was a doubt about the figures, 'we believe there might be 15,000 persons present, the shew of private carriages was scanty. Special trains brought several thousands from Lincoln, Nottingham, Leicester, &c., and the surrounding villages sent their proportion.'

Derby Racecource, established in about 1845. The grandstand was designed later, in 1852, by Henry Duesbury and replaced in 1911. Derbyshire Cricket Club were also based here from 1871. (Courtesy: Derby Local Studies Library)

There were spring and autumn meetings and by February 1856 Derby boasted a fine Dickensian grandstand designed by the architect of the Guildhall, Henry Duesbury. Races were run for the Scarsdale Stakes, the Harrington Plate, the Midland Steeplechase and the 'Selling Plate' over 'six flights of hurdles'. An advertisement in the *Mercury* pronounced: 'stakes and forfeits to be paid to the Clerk of the course, at the King's Head Hotel, Derby, before eleven o'clock of the forenoon of the day of running. No gambling booths, or play of any description allowed on the ground. Persons on horseback will not be allowed to go over the fences or beyond the winning field. All the running ground and every fence may be seen from the new Race Stand.' As it turned out the latter was 'liberally patronised' as was the enclosure and 'there was a good attendance of "professionals" from London, who availed themselves of the express train, to run down into the country'. Besides the likes of Lord Cavendish, the Earl of Chesterfield (Bretby Hall), the Earl of Harrington and Lady Ann

Chandos-Pole (Radbourne Hall), there was 'a good sprinkling of county and borough gentlemen'. By August that year the grandstand boasted a 'handsome clock' presented and fitted up by 'Mr Roskell, of Liverpool, and who is now proprietor of the late Mr Whitehurst's clock manufactory in Derby'. Also, 'additional accommodation was provided for jockeys and owners of horses by a private room being placed at their disposal'.

By 1867 there was also a summer meeting. A *Mercury* report in August noted a change for the worse in the character of support: 'The Derby Races have attracted that singular mixture of aristocratic sportsman, professional gamblers, and the inordinate quantity of blackguardism maybe found at any popular meeting'. The paper compared the occasion unfavourably with the races of 1793 when it claimed there was 'genuine racing'; the stakes were small and 'the sport real'. But there was also a rider: 'we may add that the stewards announced that there would be "Assemblies, plays, cockings, &c., as usual"', a reminder of bad old days of unashamed blood sports that the Victorians congratulated themselves on having put behind them for good. Back to August 1867: there was a sequel to the present-day meeting. The following week two men were charged with gambling on the course, presiding at 'a table with 10 horses figured thereon and a number of cards', taking bets from little boys. The odds quoted were three to one in the hosts' favour. Though they pleaded that they were allowed to do it at Nottingham they were given 14 days' gaol.

While the *Mercury* gave no detail about the amount of money the jockeys competed for, back in 1793 it was a simple case of £50 a race, while in 1838 at the Siddals it had come down to '2 sovs.' (sovereigns). But there was no doubting the climb back and beyond by October 1878 when the racecorse staged a 'Two Mile Race for £200'. There was a 'somewhat large attendance' and 'the betting fraternity from Sheffield, Notts, Staffordshire, Birmingham, Wolverhampton, and neighbouring counties was well represented'. The autumn session in November 1897 was due to be patronised by the Prince of Wales (the future King Edward VII), an avid collector of prestigious social occasions of all kinds, but Derby was disappointed through the intervention of a royal death, that of the Duchess of Teck. Even so, 'the company in the County Stand was a brilliant and distinguished one'. The Derby Cup 'attracted a field of 17', including 'many of the best handicap horses of the day' and there were even 20 entries for the Markeaton Stakes. That was on the Friday, with the largest attendance for the middle day of three now. But the turnstile arrangement let the show down somewhat, since those who had hoped to see the first race of the day 'were kept five or 10 minutes crushed and almost suffocated in the midst of "the madding crowd" before they could secure admission. Outside the rings the light-fingered gentry were conspicuous by their presence, and the "three card trick" professors carried on a roaring trade. The inevitable umbrella kept popping up at every turn only to disappear with even greater rapidity whenever the men in blue hove in sight.' *Mercury* readers were supplied with graphic illustrative material. A friend of the reporter pointed out a man looking for all the world like a well-to-do farmer but who in reality was:

… acting as a 'decoy duck' for the 'sharps'. Another thief we meet is the 'sporting gent' who has just come out of the ring with some information of an extraordinary nature about a horse 'in the next race', and who introduces himself by borrowing your pencil in order that he can mark his card. If you will give him anything from five shillings upwards he will get your money on at a far better price in the ring than you can outside – and never return with it.

Happy days! Prince Bertie disappointed the Derby racing fraternity again in November 1900 but that gathering was still, according to the *Mercury,* 'one of the most brilliant ever held in the Midlands. The Duke and Duchess of Devonshire at Chatsworth and many of the local nobility and gentry entertained large and distinguished house parties, and the general public patronised the meeting as they always do – splendidly.' A 'bright and animated' atmosphere pervaded the members' enclosure and paddock. The Duke's horse won a race on the Thursday to great acclaim, though he had to miss out on the Saturday to attend a Cabinet meeting in London! Nevertheless, ordinary folk turned up in their thousands on their half-holiday.

For perspiration's sake

There were many other leisure pursuits that required greater personal effort on the part of participants, though spectators, if fewer in number on most occasions, were naturally also excused the sweat. 'Footraces' appear to have been particularly popular in early Victorian days on the same principle as for horses. At 11 o'clock on a Monday morning in March 1838 a Derby jeweller and tailor competed 'over six score yards for £5 a-side' before 'an immense concourse of people' on the London Road 'a little below the Infirmary'. After the pistol-shot start the jeweller won by almost seven yards to the 'great disappointment of his opponent and friends'. In the *Mercury*'s judgement 'it is evident he is not so swift a runner as was anticipated'. The victor, Edward Richardson, took on a champion from Arnold, Nottingham, a month later, over a distance of 'five score yards', again on Derby's London Road, and the contest was the subject of huge interest across both counties. Though billed for a two o'clock start, 'soon after breakfast, people from various quarters began to flock in'. The result looked to the *Mercury* reporter like a dead heat, but was given to the Arnold man, though Richardson had been the favourite with plenty of his fellow jewellers' 'gold dust' resting on him winning. The paper thought Richardson had been too confident at the early stage of the race, had run carelessly, and had possibly been taught a lesson not to repeat the tactic 'when bets to a large amount depend upon him'.

By 1888 running seems to have become a club activity. That October the *Mercury* reported on the St John's Harriers, who 'turned out nine members for a slow run, proceeding through Mackworth, Langley, Radbourne, across to Etwall, Mickleover, and home, Bancroft being pacemaker. The committee hope that all members will turn up to the evening runs, so that they may turn out good teams for matches arranged.' And in November 1897 L. Eglinton, 'Captain Derby and County A. and C.C.Hrs. [Harriers]', wrote a letter of complaint to the editor drawing attention to difficulties his men faced on their outings. They had:

> ... been subjected to much annoyance from the youngsters using the West End Recreation Ground [Mr Mundy of Markeaton Hall's recent gift to the town]. The wild shouts and rude remarks they don't mind, but they object strongly to the salvoes of grass sods, lobster tins, &c., which some of the urchins hurl at them from behind

London Road at night with its tram-lines from the 1880s from just past the Spot. Fifty years earlier from beyond the far rise footraces were all the rage. (Courtesy: Derby Studies Library)

the shelter of the high palisades. This must be stopped, and I crave a little of your valuable space in the hope that the parents of the lads will see these lines, and give their children a lively warning.

Early Victorian times were, too, the age of prize-fighting, though illegal. One event took place just outside Derby on Sinfin Moor in November 1856. Thomas Whiting, alias 'Paddy Whiting' of Derby took on a man from Birmingham for '£10 a-side'. The town's superintendent of police had been tipped off and he and two constables found 'the ropes and stakes pitched, and the men stripped for the fight' as they spied from a hedge-bottom hide-out. However, one of the supporters discovered them and 'the whole lot immediately decamped, leaving behind them their "colours", two large blankets'. The chase went through Chellaston, Weston-on-Trent, Aston and Shardlow, but the fighters and their followers got safely across the Leicestershire border to set up another ring and proceed with the fight beyond the reach of the Derby police.

Ten years previously, in July 1846, an afternoon contest at Littleover for 'a sovereign a-side' had actually ended with a death. A Derby man 'we believed was named Clarke' died the evening of the battle 'of the bruises he received in the contest'. And a week later on the other side of town at Horsley the villagers were 'frightened from their propriety' by a crowd of very ruffianly fellows who fixed upon a field near the village, for one of those 'beastly scenes known as a prize fight'. A Derby man 'furiously assaulted' the owner of the land when he politely requested them to remove themselves. The local constable was also 'repeatedly assaulted'. The fighters themselves, one from Derby and the other from Nottingham, 'were dreadfully cut and knocked about'. According to the *Mercury* 'several persons had barrels of ale and liquors on the ground' and there was a rumour that a London reporter was in attendance! Windows in neighbouring cottages were smashed. Not a nice occasion at all!

A very different show of physical prowess was available in the middle of town by 1867. In October that year the Derby Gymnasium and Athletic Club 'invited their friends to witness numerous feats of strength and agility' at 'their Room, in St Mary's Gate'. The *Mercury* reported the friends 'must have been gratified and amused by what they saw. Messrs. Walker

The Free Baths at Bass Recreation Ground, probably in the 1880s. These open-air baths had two pools each 100 x 50ft and in all 129 dressing cubicles. They opened in 1873. (Courtesy: Derby Local Studies Library)

and Biggs hopped and skipped about a couple of chairs in almost all conceivable directions very spiritedly, and avoided, what to an unpractised eye seemed inevitable, the peeling of their shins'. The report added that another of the club's activities, boxing, 'in the presence of so large a number of the gentler sex, was wisely omitted.' Another pair of members proved expert trapeze artists, rewarded with 'the wondering up-turned eyes of the astonished audience'. The paper hoped the show would excite 'a sufficiently strong spirit of emulation in the minds of many young men to induce them to join the club, and take part in its very useful and invigorating exercises'.

By this time too the town provided for another kind of club athleticism in the shape of the Corporation Baths in Full Street in the shadow of All Saints'. In July 1897 the *Mercury* reported on the opening gala of the Derby Swimming Club on a Monday evening, accounted 'a great success, both as regards the number present and the carrying out of the lengthy and excellent programme that had been provided', for which the paper congratulated the presiding committee. The report added:

> His Worship the Mayor presided, and in opening the proceedings said the teaching of the art of swimming really deserved every encouragement that could be given it; it was very conducive to health, a very manly [!] exercise and sport, and it tended to promote cleanliness of body. It was also very useful in that it gave a man the means of saving the valuable lives of his fellow-creatures.

Ladies, presumably, were as yet required to look on, though in a few years' time new baths in Reginald Street would set times aside for their benefit.

Entertainment on the Derwent

Water provided for leisure in this most inland of towns in another way. The River Derwent just to the north of the middle of Derby is wide enough and sufficiently weir-free for boats to be deployed in competition. Twenty years before the Great Northern Railway crossed the river on iron ribs between Strutt's Park and Chester Green in 1877, the Derwent Rowing Club set up on the west bank. Two years after the railway crossing was made a second club, the Derby Town, was established on the opposite eastern bank just north of the bridge itself. So it was the membership of the Derwent Club that had to negotiate with the Railway Company over the design of the bridge, a fact mentioned by the club captain in May 1897 at a Thursday evening meeting 'in the Grand Jury-room of the Guildhall' over a proposal to resurrect the Derby Regatta. This had been a prestigious event for the riverside community in former years. Mr S. Abbott retold for the benefit of the meeting the story of 20 years back to put the Great Northern in a favourable light after they had presumably come in for criticism for more recent further work over the water, which called for another temporary bridge that had put a stop to rowing for two seasons and had led to Derby rowers going to other river-towns to win prizes. Of the original bridge-work of 1877 Mr Abbott said:

> So far from being concerned in any obstruction to the regatta, they had been very liberal in providing a bridge, which would allow of any regatta to take place with the

same facility as any place in England. The first design of the bridge which passed Parliament had two pillars in the river, which might have obstructed the river very much indeed, but on matters being represented to them they decided to have a structure with a clear span of 120 feet.

A Town Club member recalled that in the 1880s 'the Derby Regatta had attracted crews from Oxford, Cambridge, London, Worcester, Chester and Burton'. Resuscitation was duly resolved on, to take place at the end of July, and the Mayor added that 'he should be doubly glad if in succeeding years they had on the heights above the river in Strutt's Park, large crowds of the townspeople looking at the races from their own ground (Applause)'. However, it was not until Edwardian times that the event regained its former prestige.

The Derwent (1857) and Derby Town (1879) Rowing Clubs with the GNR bridge beyond, the design of which was modified at the request of the clubs. The Derby clubhouse was originally situated on the opposite Chester Green bank of the river. (Photo: Andrew Butterton)

By 1897 the Town Club boasted '70–80 members' but of course it was the rival Derwent Club that had the longer history. Ten years before that started there was obviously interest in using the river for sport, as in July 1846 when the *Mercury* reported on a:

ROWING MATCH ON THE RIVER DERWENT, FOR FIFTY POUNDS. This match, which has created great interest in the aquatic circles of this and the neighbouring counties, came off yesterday (Tuesday). The start was from the Darley Bar, by report of pistol. An excellent band of music was engaged, and the whole affair was a most attractive one; a great concourse of persons being present to witness the trial of skill.

Derby beat Nottingham by 'two heats to one', presumably in the final. By 1867 the Derwent Club had established a racing routine along the bottom of beauteous Darley Park, then the territory of Lord Belper of the Strutt dynasty. In April that year the paper gave an account of their opening contest:

> The 'University Day', chosen by Oxford and Cambridge, was the day fixed upon by the local white and blue, for the races by which they open their aquatic programme. The weather has not been very favourable for training: the course was often of late very 'lumpy', and more than once the crews have been literally 'waved' off the river. Making allowances for this formidable drawback we must admit that the rivals went well to the post, and that their performances were better than we had any right to expect.

The club also had a thriving social aspect, with an annual outing to Swarkestone where according to the *Mercury* they were 'received with hearty welcome'. A week after the opening races, 'several crews rowed [by river/canal or both?] from Derby, and other members came by road. A very agreeable entertainment was enjoyed at Mrs Adams's, and according to custom the party was distinguished for its exuberant fun.' In late September they conducted their 'closing races' of the year, which were 'rowed up the Derwent from St Mary's Bridge. The lowering clouds in the morning did not offer much enticement for the ladies who so ardently support the club, but the attendance was, nevertheless, of a most encouraging character, and testified to the interest which is evoked by the contests, and is manifested by the invigorating practice of rowing. The band of the Derby Volunteers played upon the ground, and secured the approbation of the spectators.'

The club was still going strong in 1897 when their opening matches took place over 'the three-quarters of a mile course'. Captain Abbott was backed up by 'a very energetic committee' from which the *Mercury* looked in the future to 'something a little more pretentious in the shape of an entertaining regatta'. They now had two new boats and entertainment was considered good: 'the Militia Band, under Bandmaster M'Carthy, played a good selection of pieces in the Boat House Field during the races. In the evening the members dined together at the Bell Hotel, when a most harmonious and convivial evening was spent'. Their closing event at the end of September 'at the field by Darley Grove' proved a disappointment, however, owing to that celestial ring-master of all outdoor occasions, the weather:

> … the spectators were very few in number. No sooner had the first race been disposed of than a series of heavy thunderstorms made the spot a most uncomfortable one, but the various contests were pursued with great heartiness and eagerness in the interval between four and six o'clock when another heavy shower caused a further interruption.

At the beginning of the month the *Mercury* had reported on their rivals' closing races, which were also in a suffering condition. Only three crews could turn out because of holidays and the river was 'in a very swollen state owing to the recent rains'.

By 1867 the Derby Regatta had established itself as an important annual event in the town calendar through 'energetic management' by the committee responsible, which must at that time have been dominated by members of the older club. The one in July 1867 was reported 'to have eclipsed all its forerunners and induces a reasonable expectation that the local river races will speedily possess much more than a local interest'. It attracted competitors from Nottingham and Burton, to whom, as we have seen, several others had been added by the 1880s. However, there were no outsiders for the Junior fours race in 1867 – Derby School day boys easily beat the boarders. St Mary's RC boat beat Derwent for the Corporation Plate but then lost to Burton for the Ladies' Plate. Dinner at the Bell followed in the evening.

Free-wheeling

Rowing, even solo, was essentially a club activity unless the enthusiast had a house beside a river or lake where, like the young William Wordsworth, he could 'take wing' with boat and oar when it pleased him. But by the 1880s there was a machine available that liberated the individual man and, even more so, woman from the confines of first detached and later terraced houses as never before and provided the healthiest exercise possible in doing so. The day of the bicycle had arrived. It could be used in company, and competitively by joining a club, and Derby boasted early examples of the latter. But it must have been the joy of individual free movement that gripped first, sheer poetry of motion.

And of course the opportunity was there as never before to enjoy the glories of Derby's surroundings. At the end of March 1897 the *Mercury*'s cycling correspondent waxed poetic

Bridge over the Markeaton Brook, one of the spots on the edge of Derby easily accessible to cyclists from the 1880s. (Photo: Dr Frank Jones)

in his/her seasonal message, which, after Shakespearean flights, required a come-down of pure bathos:

> It will be some time before the leaves of the forest trees begin to unroll, but the hedgerows are already green, and the floral procession has begun. The scented violet and the pallid primrose have made their appearance, and the wayside bank is an index of coming beauty. Spotted and shiny arums, deeply indented wild parsley, purple-veined dock, soft-grey foxgloves, leaves of ground ivies, of celandine, wood-violets, dandelion, Jack-by-the-hedge, herb-robert all foretell the return of the wild flowers to their accustomed quarters. Springtime has come, and now is the time for cyclists to put a girdle round as much of the earth as they possibly can.

By May the call to the narrow saddle had obviously been heard abundantly:

> A more perfect day for cycling than May Day would be difficult to imagine. Roads, which earlier in the week had been rather dusty, were in capital condition; a westerly wind tempered the sun's rays, which lighted up a countryside which at present is surpassingly beautiful, and the consequence was that most of the roads were alive with wheelmen and wheelwomen, many of them bent on rural retreats which lie far off the highways.

By summer, Derbyshire had become Shangri-La:

> … the lanes and bye-ways provide much the most interesting riding. The highways are so busy on fine afternoons that it is a positive relief to turn away from beaten tracts to where the novice ceases troubling and the lurcher is not. Moreover, hedge-backings are bright with many flowers, while the air is heavy-laden with ambrosial new cut hay, mingled with the scent of the honeysuckle. And there are shaded corners there to be found where you may while away the happy hours, the while the scorcher, who never deserts the broad surface of the high road, gets done to death with the sun's hot rays.

There were, indeed, difficulties to be overcome. That June, the *Mercury* cycling column quoted at length an article in a specialist journal to the effect that while the Derby cyclist had almost under the handlebars 'some of the wildest and remote moorland scenery to be found in all England in the Peak Districts', the weather could be treacherous. The writer added:

> … under the influence of rain Derbyshire roads are absolutely the worst I have ever sampled. The slimiest slime that ever accumulates on town setts is not more suggestive of side-slipping than a Derbyshire road undergoing the drying process after rain, and not only so, but the surface 'picks up' in lumps to freely decorate one's person and add pounds of useless weight to rider and machine.

All the same, by then the new craze had the blessing of the Church in the person of the Bishop of Lichfield who, writing in the previous month's issue of the *Rambler* magazine, endorsed the welcome he'd heard the Dean of Rochester give to cyclists attending his cathedral's Sunday service. He went on: 'The cyclist, except to obtain necessary refreshments, gives no work or trouble to anyone; he looks after his machine himself, and cleans it himself at the close of the day. Anything that helps him to mark his Sunday as the Lord's Day is to be welcomed.' Specialist cycle shops were obviously in the future but the activity was certainly good for the ladies, though apparently not in the Bishop's survey. A Mrs Longshore-Potts gave a lecture at the Grand Theatre in Derby in September 1897 on a Thursday afternoon in which she declared cycling 'a godsend to her sex' but was less than wild about the way they dressed for it! She didn't care for the remedy the pundits were pushing in order to avoid 'a wide skirt lifting and flapping in the wind', and she added that if women 'could not cycle without a loss of feminine grace they should not cycle at all'. Her target audience must have been a middle-class one and the timing of her lecture would hardly have allowed Derby millgirls to attend! This does indeed prompt reflection as to how many working-class people, male or female, could have afforded a machine before the last few years of the century. Possibly not many, a conclusion that seems to be confirmed by a hint, no more, in an article by the *Mercury*'s editor in the same year attempting to summarise the changes that had taken place during the Queen's reign.

The individual cyclist could achieve wonders. In October 1900 a Derby man, Robert N. Cary, knocked 3 minutes 54 seconds off the world record (5 hours 30 minutes) for 100 miles distance. The location of this feat was the London to Bath Road and the champion was 22 years old and nearly 6ft 6in in height! He must have achieved this record on the basis of club membership. There was a Derby Bicycle Club as early as 1878, but it obviously faced opposition from elderly backwoodsmen if the new machines were deployed on the town streets. In March that year the *Mercury* published a letter signed simply 'H.F.G.' in which the writer stated that he had declined an invitation to become a member, despite the fact that its vice-president was none other than the Revd W. Chandos-Pole, because he was 'neither a young man nor a fast one' and so its encouragement of 'athletic exercises and sanitary progress' was wasted on him! However, he did declare himself impressed by the club. It had both a surgeon and a chaplain – a back-hander, as he took it as an admission of a need for 'surgical aid and religious consolation'! He went on at some length to place the simple bike alongside other Victorian transport inventions:

These modern velocipedes require a jockey of skill to ride them. The iron-horse might be very safe up Green-hill and very dangerous down St Peter's incline. I fear the School Board would not undertake the training of these aspiring townsmen, as no ordinary jockey could keep his seat and safely steer these impetuous dreadnoughts. The Sanitary Board do not approve of Bicycles in the streets, as they are a dangerous nuisance. I have several times encountered disagreeable alarm from these silent locomotives; they come upon one as suddenly as a thief in the dark, and for a moment one scarcely knows whether an arm or a foot has been severed from the entire body, though the result may only prove what doctors call 'a shock to the nervous system'! I cannot conceive a more ignoble death than being wheeled over by a ferocious bicycle, or mutilated by an omnibus, or life stamped out by a tram carriage, and finally flattened by a steam roller.

The proper place for the bike was the park to this observer, since as exercise cycling bore 'no comparison with walking, running, cricketing, racketing, boating, or horse-riding'. If the bike could be trained to go cross-country after hounds it might be useful! He obviously couldn't see far enough into the future, though perhaps the combination of cycle plus expensive gearing and robust tyres minus the fox could open up undreamed of possibilities yet in the early 21st century!

Nevertheless the clubs flourished. In late September 1878 they had a showcase in 'the field adjoining the Arboretum' in the form of 'a great bicycle meeting' attended by up to 1,300 people according to the *Mercury*. There were contests for amateurs and professionals. Among the latter was current world champion Keen, who 'possesses an easy and graceful seat, which is quite sufficient to make one enamoured of the art of propelling the machine.' Exactly what did our reporter mean, one wonders! In the final Keen 'soon demolished the 350 yards which separated him from his opponents, and increased the distance with every revolution. Finally he won by nearly half-a-mile.' But Derby's Rowson at least came second, 40 yards ahead of the third man, a Londoner.

By 1897 club routine was well established. From Good Friday on it was the touring season, 'the first social gathering out of doors', though there were indeed earlier runs 'to get riders' limbs and mind in better order' and 'the bearings and saddle of the machine in easy going condition'. In March that year the *Mercury* published the Derby Castle Fields Cycling Club's weekly Saturday and Sunday programme of runs for April to Burton (combining with Derby Rovers and Fletcher's CC), Duffield, Kegworth, Sawley, Matlock, Etwall, Brailsford, Loughborough and Charnwood, Melbourne and Castle Donnington and Sandiacre. That May the paper gave a glimpse of the experience of one such run, just as novelist Thomas Hardy and composer Edward Elgar, bike fans both, rode their machines further south in Dorset and Worcester, where enclosing mills were few and far between:

> Lovely summer weather favoured the members of the Castle Fields Cycling Club for their run to Via Gellia on Saturday last. Thirty started from head quarters shortly after 2pm, and the party put up for refreshments at Whatstandwell, the Derwent Hotel. Via Gellia was reached at about 4.30, arrangements having previously been made for tea at the cottage. Afterwards the wheelmen spent their time in the lovely valley gathering ferns and lilies and meeting again for the return journey at the Pig of Lead. Derby was reached at about 8.30, everyone being delighted at their peep at picturesque Derbyshire.

Some members on that expedition might also have enjoyed the joke the *Mercury* pinched for its March issue from a cycling magazine and alleged to be current 'in at least three continents', about 'a waggish climber having decorated a precipice on Mont Blanc with the notice, 'This hill is dangerous for cyclists'.

Mackworth Castle, another easily accessible spot in the surrounding countryside for town cyclists. (Photo: Dr Frank Jones)

As a postscript to this account of life on two wheels we might briefly mention locomotion on four unaided by the power of one or more of mankind's so-called best friends. We have already noted the motor car's arrival on the Derby scene with an Auto-mobile Club test run at the end of April 1900 and how another of the more conservative citizens of the town might have had enough of the wondrous smelly new machines particularly if a dog-lover. Seventy vehicles had started from London but 12 had broken down before getting as far as Birmingham. Car makes identified in the report, in fact the fastest two up Taddington Hill, the most taxing incline on the whole trip later on that afternoon, were an Ariel Tricycle and a Panhard with one C.S. Rolls at the wheel.

Bat and Ball

The male of the species preferred to take his exercise in far greater numbers, in Derby as elsewhere, confined to a single expansive green space. Before Derbyshire Cricket Club gave birth to the Rams in the early 1880s the sound of willow applied to a leather sphere was the sonic poetry shared by more teams and clubs than any other kind. The obsession could annoy others, as a *Mercury* report of a meeting of the Town Council at the Guildhall in August 1846 tells us. Councillor Madeley voiced complaints that the Holmes, which 20 years later was bought for the town by Thomas Bass, was barred to ordinary folk unless they paid an entrance fee when there was a Derby Town cricket match going on. The club paid £25 a year for a portion of the space in the absence of a proper cricket ground. Indeed the Holmes was the scene of other cricketing contests, such as the one on a Monday in August 1856 'among the members of the police force, who had received permission from the authorities for a day's recreation. The weather was tolerably fine, and the match was conducted in a manner gratifying alike to the winners and those whom the fortune of the day doomed to defeat.' The same space was also used by the Derbyshire County Club, as on a Tuesday and Wednesday back in July 1846 when the home side mauled Leicestershire by an innings and 26 runs. The game was apparently too one-sided for many spectators, though on the second day 'some of the leading families of the neighbourhood were present in their carriages'.

In 1867 the Town Club was established in a new ground on City Road, Chester Green. According to a report in May this was 'in splendid condition, considering the short time it has been made, and it bids fair to be excelled by few in the Midland Counties; it is most pleasantly situated, adjacent to the River Derwent, and commands a beautiful prospect for miles around Derby'. This presents a puzzle for us today with its reference to an extensive view, though Parker's Piece, which seems to be indicated and where the attractive pavilion was added in

A corner of Chester Green where Derby Town Cricket Club established a new playing ground much admired in 1867. The Green, declared a Public Recreation Ground a few years later, featured in the Jubilee celebrations of 1897. (Photo: Andrew Butterton)

1886, would not at the earlier date have been enclosed by terraced housing away from the river and by the mighty Haslam works of the 1870s on the town side. Whatever, the town club had a healthy following, reminding us that until well after World War Two entertainment, live or screen-simulated, was in comparatively short supply: 'There were a large number of spectators on the ground, which added a lively appearance to the game, and went to prove the interest that has in years past been manifested in the game of cricket by the Derby people is still felt.' The club, which did battle with neighbouring village sides, had its first annual dinner in October 1867 at the County Hotel. The evening was distinguished by a fine old buffer of a speech by Colonel Wilmot VC, its president. He enthused about rivalling Nottingham at last and about the traits of character developed by the 'peculiarly English game' – he defined these as 'courage, determination, quickness of perception and action, decision, and patience (Cheers)'. It had of course spread wherever Englishmen had colonised: 'he (Colonel Wilmot) had played it on the sandy plains of India, and under the walls of Pekin, and during the heat of the mutiny [India's 'War of Independence'], whenever they had one day's cessation of mutineer-hunting he took to leather-hunting (Loud cheers)'. The sportsmen ate like lords that evening as Lords Harrington and Scarsdale and Messrs Evans and Bass MPs had sent hares, pheasants, rabbits and grapes from their estates for consumption.

By 1878 the County Club had 'now fairly established itself as a cricketing shire' on the national scene, though that current season was not as successful as the previous one, with six lost games to three wins. They had played Yorkshire on a Sheffield evening after a 'storm of rain and hail', with the *Mercury* reporter commenting that 'the spectacle of the wicket-keeper kicking back the mud-covered ball to the bowler was not particularly dignified in a cricketer's eyes', and also the MCC at Lord's, London, against the legendary Dr W.G. Grace, who flayed them with both bat and ball. There were certainly ups and downs in the 1880s. A glorious

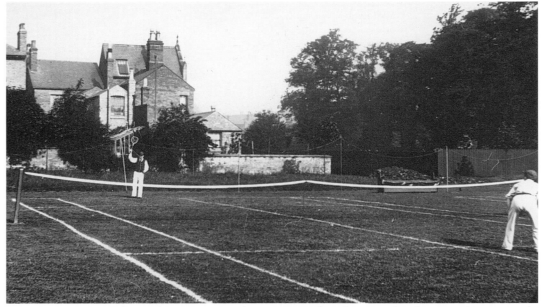

A late-Victorian alternative to outdoor team games: playing tennis in the Arboretum. Photo by Keene. (Courtesy: Derby Museums and Art Gallery)

victory over Yorkshire in 1888 was noted by the *Mercury* as Derbyshire's first win over any so-called first-class county for three whole years, though they also beat the MCC, and the paper's editor was incensed at a London journalist placing the beloved county in the second class. Worse was to come though. In 1897 they won not one game out of 16 played, with nine losses! The county was bottom of the table again in 1899 but did rather better in the final Victorian season of 1900. By then, Derbyshire possessed a batting star by the name of Storer who scored 176 against Essex. He was picked for England to tour Australia in the winter. However, the county were flogged once again by the mighty, now 58-year-old 'Dr W.G.' down in his London lair in June, but got revenge on him at Derby. He was out twice 'leg before' at the Racecourse ground for a miserable two then six and got taken to task by the *Mercury*, not that he'd care, for making it quite plain that he disagreed with umpire Sherwin's decisions in each case. This apparently was not all that surprising, since the good Doctor's patronising response to getting bowled out at any time was to put on an extremely mystified expression and mutter audibly 'Where did that one come from?'

Football progress

There was one decidedly male approach to coping with leisure time that was even more seductive than cricket. The story of 'the beautiful game' in Derby could be said to challenge the notion of 'progress' in one respect, though overall it did represent a motion along the beast to beauty tangent. How important is participation in sport? The game went from mass action in the open street and even river, Ashbourne-style, in the 1840s to the spectacle of thousands more or less passively watching the artistry of a mere 11 players at the Baseball Ground in the 1890s! And the ground wasn't constructed for football anyway, as its name implies. In August 1897 Derby won the English Baseball Cup Final at home by beating Middlesborough 30–7 after previously demolishing the Crystal Palace team. Regarding this latter match the *Mercury* commented: 'Baseball is evidently rapidly growing in popularity in Derby, and there was an attendance of over three thousand to witness the semi-final between the local club and the Crystal Palace on Saturday'.

But it was the feet-only technique that eventually swamped the male imagination. Shrovetide football itself was stamped on by the Town Council back in February 1846 as a public order matter. The *Mercury* published the decree against it, the reason given that 'the public peace is broken, the peaceable inhabitants put in great fear, property destroyed, banking-houses and shops closed, and public business suspended'. The Mayor termed the pastime 'barbarous and disgusting'; it had for many years 'annually disgraced our town'. On that particular Shrove Tuesday 'the special constables were on duty, and blocked up the different entrances to the Market Place, where the ball has always been thrown up, in order to prevent any body of men congregating there'. There was indeed expectancy in the air as 'large numbers of lads and young men thronged the streets'. A ball was in fact 'thrown up' but after being put in the river with 'hundreds' rushing after it the round object was immediately 'secured by the police, and cut in pieces'. Then, after duty constables in the Morledge were 'insulted and attacked', another ball was thrown from the door of a public house there. The Mayor was 'struck on the shoulder by a brick-bat, hurled by some ferocious ruffian, and severely bruised'. The Riot Act was read and soldiers were called in, but the participants got

The entrance to the Baseball Ground, theatre for the drama of the likes of Steve Bloomer and so many other stars before it became 'the Beautiful Game' in recent times. (Photo: Dr Frank Jones)

the ball in the Derwent for a second time and followed it downstream in the direction of the Holmes. However, on Ash Wednesday, though the streets were again 'thronged with people', the active element 'called it a day'. Those who had taken on the police were hauled before the Court. But in Ashbourne of course the action continued uninterrupted through the century with undiminished ferocity!

While the Rams (Derby County) were formed as an offshoot of the County Cricket Club in 1884, it was not they who first won glory in the regulated form of the game during that decade. In January 1888 on the Arboretum Field Derby Junction (originally a Board School team) beat the mighty Blackburn Rovers 2–1 in the quarter-finals of the FA Cup, though their opponents protested about the quality of the pitch. Sadly Junction lost to West Bromwich in the semi-finals and the following year were knocked out of the competition early on by the Rams and ceased to exist a few years later. It was Derby County that took part in the inaugural season of the Football League in 1888, though that December they were beaten 2–1 by another Derby team, the Midland (the 'railwaymen'). From that season on the Rams alone played with the elite, having even in the same breath as losing to the Midland beaten such illustrious names as Bolton Wanderers, Blackburn Rovers and Wolves. By 1896 it was the Rams' turn to reach the Cup semi-final, a feat they repeated the following year after beating Newton Heath (now Manchester United no less!), who were obviously considered 'pond life' as according to the *Mercury* 'Derby had a much harder struggle than their supporters anticipated'.

So it was to Stoke for the big game against Everton in March 1897. There was a great crowd of nearly 20,000 'which the Pottery football enthusiast has never seen before', swollen by numerous special rail day-excursions, especially along the GNR and North Staffs lines. The Beaconsfield (Conservative) Club in Derby hired 'two sumptuous saloons' on the 12.50 from

Friar Gate Station, the Derby County team itself having travelled on the 11am North Staffs train. Derby, who had been beaten at the same stage the previous year, were this time favourites. They had a star goalscorer in Steve Bloomer. But they lost again 3–2, largely, according to the *Mercury,* because they had only 10 men for at least half the game since until well after World War Two no substitutes were allowed in the case of injury to a player. Also, both Bloomer and goalkeeper Robinson, internationals both, 'were not up to their usual form'. In fact Bloomer scored for England against Scotland a fortnight later, though he again found himself on the losing side.

Rams supporters might have noticed this mighty GNR warehouse in pristine condition on setting out from Friar Gate for Stoke in 1897. (Photo: Andrew Butterton)

But the Rams would glory in that season's record if it could be repeated today! They were third in the League, after being second the previous season, winning 16 games against 10 losses. In the last of all Victorian seasons they finished sixth. There was then a depressed feeling about as, reported the *Mercury,* the Boer War 'has made its influence felt everywhere, and the interest taken in football has been far less than usual. Nearly every big club has the same complaint to make.' In a Cup tie against Sunderland at Derby the Rams were winning comfortably 'until a terrific snowstorm broke over the town and made accurate football impossible'. At Sunderland, a game was stopped 10 minutes from time with the Rams leading and had to be replayed. Then the old, old story – the referee made some 'marvellous decisions' at Birmingham to give Aston Villa a lucky win. Ill fortune continued into the beginning of the following campaign in September 1900 when Derby lost 1–0 to Newcastle, when the referee blew the last whistle just as Bloomer was putting the ball into the opposition net. Finally, that

Steve Bloomer, possibly the Rams' greatest-ever player. (Courtesy: W.W. Winter)

December Bloomer hit the Everton crossbar three times with shots a sports journalist judged 'the custodian could never have seen' before the Merseysiders scored! So at the end of the century the *Mercury*'s verdict was that 'the County may feel legitimately aggrieved at the unkindness of Dame Fortune'.

For those indoors

There was plenty on offer for Derbeians for whom outdoor pursuits were not a first consideration, both in the way of entertainment and individual activity. For all the family there was the occasional circus, which at least in early Victorian times seems to have provided more distraction than it does today. We have seen elsewhere that the Victorians, though originating organisations like the RSPCA, had not quite developed a sharp conscience about caging and controlling large animals. So in January 1846 a *Mercury* reporter paid a visit to 'Hughes' Circus', described as 'this place of entertainment' and so possibly posing a question as to whether the show was a touring affair or something more permanent in the town. At any rate it had a following, as it 'continues to attract numerous and fashionable audiences'. It featured on one evening 'Mr W.O. Dale, the star rider of America', performing 'some of the most extraordinary feats ever witnessed, whilst the horse was at full speed'. Another evening was taken with 'the grand equestrian spectacle of Timour the Tartar. The piece was produced on a scale of grandeur that was never before attempted in this town, and reflects great credit on the management of Mr Hughes.' Four Egyptian camels were 'harnessed to a splendid car' and pulling Timour and Princess Zorilda in it. The proprietor and his wife appeared on horseback too 'as the Swiss milkmaid and Tyrolean shepherd'.

The Corn Exchange, venue for a variety of shows from the 1860s on. (Photo: Andrew Butterton)

In January 1856 it was the turn of Hengler's Circus, performing in Albert Street. Where exactly the *Mercury* doesn't specify. It may have been on the site of the Corn Exchange, which became a popular place for shows when completed five years later. Open space must have been required, because the report mentions a building 'substantially erected, and the inside has a very tasteful and comfortable appearance', which possibly suggests the company brought it with them. The act that seems to have made the biggest impact was Signor Russilli and a boy of between nine and 12 years of age called 'the Pine Mounter or Mid-air Contortionist', who climbed up a pole held up by his master and spun round at the top 'with an ease and grace that lessens the trepidation generally felt by those witnessing such acts'. Much more demeaning to animals, however, was the visiting show in October the same year, 'Mander's Collection of Wild Beasts', which were displayed in the Market on a Thursday evening. The animals 'in first-rate condition' were accompanied by a brass band! Indoors, a 'lion-slayer' put 'the lords of the forest', as his hand-outs promised, through 'a variety of surprising manoeuvres' inside their cage, finishing with 'an imitation lion-fight and capture'. The audience were astounded by 'the complete control he had over the animals, and loudly applauded the feat'.

Theatrical evenings

The Theatre Royal in Bold Lane was the place to go in early Victorian times for a staged experience. On the evidence of a letter published by the *Mercury* in February 1846 from a country vicar protesting about the sort of thing that went on there it had recently been reopened. In fact, back in March 1837 the paper announced that the theatre had been 'newly painted, embellished and decorated throughout by Mr Stamford, Artist', and more recently in January 1846 that it had been, in the words of the actor-manager J. Faucet Saville, 'thoroughly renovated, and many improvements and additions made to the comfort of the audience'. It had started life in the previous century and closed down again finally in the 1860s. 'Clericus', as the vicar signed himself, declared the theatre was a source of 'sorrow and vexation' to 'all friends of religion and morality'. An evening spent there was the ruination of poor young country girls who hadn't the means of choosing the company they kept. He bracketed the theatre in this respect with the racecourse. He was replied to the following week in no uncertain terms by the manager, who maintained his fellow thespians were as moral as any other group of people and more charitable than most! How typical the cleric's views were is impossible to say.

Interestingly, in October that year the *Mercury* advertised the shows at the Theatre Royal in conjunction with the Derby Races and under the patronage of the Race Stewards. The bill of fare was decidedly on the lightweight side: after the famous classic comedy *She Stoops To Conquer*, there was a musical touch with 'the Laughable Entertainment of THE SPOILED CHILD'. Miss Kate Saville, presumably the manager's wife or daughter, would play the part of Little Pickle and sing various, again presumably popular, ditties. The evening would conclude with 'the popular Farce of THE RACE BALL; OR CHAOS IS COME AGAIN'. Which surely did seem 'par for the course'! On the occasion of the renovations in 1837 and at the beginning of 1846 mentioned previously the shows advertised were 'the popular Melo-Drama, LUKE THE LABOURER' followed by 'a variety of SINGING and DANCING', then 'Sheridan Knowles's play of The Hunchback and the favourite farce of A Rowland for an Oliver' (1846).

There was a further subject of complaint in May 1856. A W.F. Wilkinson protested about the lurid poster advertisement for the current production, 'a terrific drama in three acts (never acted here) entitled The Poisoner, founded upon the poisonings committed in Paris by Madame Laffarge, and bearing great similitude to the Rugeley Poisonings now occupying the attention of the United Kingdom' – and which surely would have formed a current topic of gossip in Iron Gate or the Corn Market! The correspondent maintained this was 'grossly and revoltingly inhuman' since the trial was still going on. He/she added, 'Surely it must be a gratuitous insult to the lowest and coarsest portion of the Derby populace, to expect that such a performance will have any other attraction for them than the satisfaction of hissing it off the stage'!

There were, too, special occasional solo performances, like the example advertised back in October 1837 for nine-year-old 'Master B. Goldsmith' at the new Mechanics' Hall in the Wardwick. The *Mercury* described Goldsmith as 'a very interesting boy, of a pleasing intellectual countenance, and, for his age, an extraordinary prodigy'. His act was to play 'above FORTY CHARACTERS' with full dress and scenery. He would be at Derby on his way north to Sheffield. The advertisement concluded: 'To commence at Eight o'clock. Carriages to be ordered at 10.'

By the 1870s the Theatre Royal had closed its doors and the Corn Exchange in Albert Street had taken its place. In May 1878 Shakespeare's *Henry V* was on, possibly signalling a change of taste towards the more serious side of the dramatic spectrum and a move towards a hiving off of the more comic and mixed-media song and dance routines to the Music Hall of late Victorian days. The company playing at the Corn Exchange was headed by a famous tragic actor of the day, 'Mr John Coleman', with 'dresses and scenes said to be archaeologically correct'. The modern mania for 'conceptual' productions had mercifully not yet gripped! In October the Exchange hosted a touring production of *Uncle Tom's Cabin* with several 'coloured people' as actors. The *Mercury* declared, 'The entertainment is of so novel a character that we strongly advise our readers to take the present opportunity of witnessing it'. In December it was the turn of pantomime – *Aladdin*. The paper again enticed with praise for the scenery which 'generally will be found to exceed expectations, and the representation of the city of Pekin [Beijing], illuminated for a fete, is really very good indeed'. Above all, Pekin, Beijing or no, it would be found to be delightfully local in parts, with the opportunity never missed of getting at the Council, as in Scene ix:

BADROULBADOUR – And you will live here, dear Aladdin?
ALADDIN – Yes, And livery servants in most gorgeous dresses
Shall wait upon you – you shall hear the lark
Sing from your palace in Sim's Park.
BAD. – I thought Parks the peoples' – their estates.
ALAD. – The people are allowed to pay the rates.
BAD. – The rates are high, yet people pay.
ALAD. – They do;
And with *high rates* they get *irate* too, &c.

Grand Theatre

From 1886 onwards Derby had a house for drama on a grand scale. Though impresario Andrew Melville's Grand Theatre on Babington Lane had to be rebuilt within weeks due to a disastrous fire, it quickly established itself as the jewel in the town's theatrical coronet. Its third autumn season in 1888 featured a return to his native haunts by an old boy of Derby School who had risen to fame on the London stage. Richard Mansfield was proud to acknowledge the debt he owed to his old school in catching the acting bug and, fresh from a triumph in the intriguing dual part of Dr Jekyll and Mr Hyde in the dramatised version of Robert Louis Stevenson's classic 'creepy' novel of the same name, he came to present Derby's first two performances of it to packed houses 'in aid of a fund for providing the school with a new racquet court'. The *Mercury* gloried in his 'wonderfully facile voice' in the part, 'at one time uttering the soft accents of love and at the next roaring out the exaltations of the demonic assassin'. His every move was 'followed with almost painful intensity of attention, and at the close of each act he had a unanimous call'.

And now Derby's music lovers had been provided with the stage by which they could indulge a passion for grandest opera. With the Grand Theatre present, not for them the early 21st-century trek to Nottingham's Royal Centre for a full professional performance of the three giants of the operatic world, Mozart, Verdi and Wagner. London's Carl Rosa Opera Company could come to Derbyshire with no qualms about standards. In March 1900 the boards of Melville's stage echoed to the rarified sounds of Richard Wagner's *Lohengrin* and to the debut tones in England of a noted German tenor, Herr Julius Walther, in the title role.

The Grand Theatre of 1886, creation of Andrew Melville, home to panto, plays and even Grand Opera in late-Victorian times. (Photo: Dr Frank Jones)

Ebb and flow of music

In opera, drama and music come together and this performance was like the estuary mouth of a long stream of musical appreciation and endeavour in the town from the 1830s on. Many a great performer-artist found an appreciative audience among Derbeians. For example, in October 1838 Johann Strauss the Elder, father of the composer of *The Blue Danube* and himself described in the *Mercury* as 'the celebrated Valz Composer, from Vienna', brought to Derby his 'unrivalled Orchestra composed of 28 ARTISTES'. It is somewhat of a mystery how long his visit lasted and how many performances he gave here in the brand new Lecture Hall of the Mechanics' Institute in the Wardwick. The *Mercury* gave no report of his scheduled first concert on 9 October, in which he was to 'introduce a Selection of his Compositions, as performed by him at the courts of *Austria, Prussia, France, Holland, Belgium,* and at the *Coronation* [Victoria's] *in London*'. Then on 28 November, nearly two months on, the paper published an apology from Mr Strauss deeply regretting not being able to conduct a concert the previous Monday evening through illness and being 'aware of the great disappointment that the Nobility and Gentry have experienced, but they will readily allow, that the great expense of keeping his numerous establishment at Derby, as well as disarranging every engagement on his route, would have induced him to do everything in his power to perform, if nature would have allowed'. Which does indicate the type of audience he expected to entertain! But he did declare himself well enough to conduct another concert that coming Wednesday evening (the *Mercury* came out on Wednesday mornings). Again there was no report of what happened on this occasion either.

Johann Strauss was followed two years later in September 1840 by probably the most famous and distinguished musician to visit Derby, at least in Victorian times, the virtuoso pianist-composer Franz Liszt. He played some of his own compositions on a new grand piano 'brought expressly from London for the occasion'. It had been made by the firm Erard of Paris and Liszt was obviously promoting it for them on a six-month European tour. He was also raising money for a statue of Beethoven to be put up in the great man's birthplace, Bonn. From the Wardwick he went on by coach-and-horse to Nottingham to play a second concert that day! The *Mercury*'s critic was hugely impressed with Listz's playing, which had 'the semblance of a magnificent orchestra, rather than a piano-forte display'.

In February 1856, again at the Lecture Hall, there was a recital by Jenny Lind, famous at the time as 'The Swedish Nightingale', accompanied by her husband. She had been to Derby before. This time patrons were advised that 'THE HALL WILL BE ILLUMINATED WITH GAS. Parties with carriages are requested to set down and take up with the horses' heads towards St Werburgh's Church'. This suggests an anticipated need for some sort of traffic control. Miss Lind sang taxing operatic arias and was obviously

The entrance to the Mechanics' Institution, established 1825 and improved in the 1830s and 1890s, venue for evening classes, lectures, concerts and exhibitions. (Photo: Andrew Butterton)

a huge favourite, being received with 'repeated bursts of enthusiastic applause'. Her technique sent the *Mercury* critic into raptures:

> There seems no effort on the part of the singer; yet the very absence of apparent effort increases the wonder experienced at their [the notes] surprising prolongation and at the same time the intense, absolutely painful anxiety of the hearer, as to the possibility of their being brought to a successful close. But the wonder is increased tenfold, while the anxiety is turned to the most exquisite pleasure, when after the single note has been ringing, clear yet soft, without the slightest intermission, for an almost incredible length of time, the voice glides smoothly to a half-note, and, still without any apparent effort, without any perceptible drawing in of the breath, warbles 'smoothly' on to the end of the phrase.

Not in the same league of seriousness but still inspiring astonishment on the part of the paper's critic were two blind artists who appeared at the Lecture Hall in September 1856 and May 1867 respectively. It may have been a case of a novelty element that drew the crowds on these occasions as the *Mercury* was complaining at the earlier date of poor attendance for serious concerts, even of an effort to 'revive the musical reputation once enjoyed by Derby'. At any rate on the first occasion there was undoubted acclaim for 'Picco, The Sardinian Minstrel' who was described as 'of European celebrity'. To the *Mercury* he proved 'astonishing'. On a tiny three-holed shepherd's pipe he produced:

> ... tones the power, brilliancy, variety, and rapidity of execution of which must astonish every hearer, however ignorant of, or however familiar with music as an art. The spectator sees led upon the stage a blind man, having all the awkward nervousness of a veritable peasant. He puts his hand up to his mouth – for at the distance of a few yards no one catches so much as a glimpse of the instrument itself – and at once there poured forth a perfect torrent of the most brilliantly executed and difficult music.

The second event starred 'Blind Tom', who despite his black skin, in the estimation of Derby's senior paper, was 'assuredly one of the most accomplished musicians ever heard in Derby'. On the grand piano he 'played with his left hand Kafoosebim, and with his right hand Paddle your own Canoe, whilst he sang Trab Trab'. When the faint sounds of church bells were heard, whether from St Werburgh's or All Saints', he simply responded by reproducing the tones and notes coming from outside! In March the same year, this time at the relatively new Corn Exchange in Albert Street, two famous classical names of the time appeared in concert – Charles Halle, founder of Manchester's illustrious orchestra, on the piano, and Josef Joachim, friend of the great German composer Brahms, on the violin.

The Drill Hall in Newland Street, the foundation stone ceremony of which on 3 June 1852 was witnessed by the famous Dickensian cartoonist George Cruikshank, was the favoured venue for celebrity recitals in later Victorian times. In April 1897, through the auspices of the proprietor of the local music shop in Iron Gate, Mr Charles Foulds, there was a recital by the great Polish pianist of the day, Paderewski. The Derby audience 'listened with rapt attention for two hours and a quarter'. 'The Magnetic Pole', as he was popularly known, 'played with remarkable brilliancy, and marvellous verve'. However, more external sounds, this time produced by a flock of sheep being driven to or from market past the Hall entrance, could not on this occasion be turned to advantage as Paderewski was in the middle of Beethoven's mighty *Waldstein* sonata! The *Mercury* put in a plea to the authorities to arrange for the closure of Newland Street on concert evenings.

All through Victorian times there were local orchestral concerts in Derby. In the earlier years the town's leading musician was 'Mr Glover', who led an orchestra through a range of classical works including Mozart's great *Jupiter* symphony at the Mechanics' Hall. And by November 1897 a new national music craze had hit Derby in the form of the Promenade Concert, the most famous version of which at the Albert Hall has remained to us over a century later through the sponsorship of the BBC. The *Mercury* reported on a concert in the second season of the phenomenon in the town, taken by 'Messrs. Pike and King's Band' at the Drill Hall, with half of the programme devoted to the music of Wagner! Those attending were invited to chose two items for performance at future concerts by filling in a paper slip, with the result that *William Tell* and *The Geisha* would hopefully have featured on the music stands before too long as the top choices out of 60 items returned by 400 music lovers.

Those choristers

The lasting legacy of Victorian music-making in the town is the Derby Choral Union, formed out of the regional forces that set the handsome girders of the magnificent new Market Hall resounding to the strains of Handel's *Messiah* on 29 May 1866. There had previously been a Derby Choral Society that in October 1837 had helped to celebrate the anniversary of the opening of the Derbyshire General Infirmary with a 'Grand Selection of Sacred Music'. By 1897 there was also a Derby Orpheus and Madrigal Society performing in the Temperance Hall on Curzon Street, one of whose concerts in March that year the *Mercury* believed would 'fully maintain its reputation'. There was naturally too always a healthy audience for music with a lighter touch, such as was provided by the 'Ethiopian Harmonists' in two performances a day at the Athenaeum Room and the Theatre Royal in November 1846, at which many pieces were 're-demanded' by the listeners. These singers had, according to the reporter, 'most happily designated themselves harmonists; for, in the concerted pieces their voices blended together in beautiful harmony, and produced a sweet effect. Nor must we omit to notice the performance of Buffalo Gals, the Phantom Chorus, and the Railway Overture, which greatly excited the risible faculties of the audience.' In more doubtful taste, we might strongly suspect from our present-day vantage point, would have been the Derwent Rowing Club's 'Annual Concert' in March 1856 in the Mechanics' (Lecture) Hall featuring 'Popular Entertainment by the Derwent Gentlemen Niggers'. In January 1901 at the Temperance Hall again popular ballads were the fare.

But it was the Choral Union that featured twice a year at some length in the columns of the *Mercury* for 35 years to the close of the Victorian era. It possessed 200 members for its opening season in 1867, including 'our very best singers'. There was a need, the paper's critic thought, to revive former glories 'when Derby ranked high for well-cultivated musical ability, when

The interior of the Market Hall in 1866, the virtual birthplace of Derby Choral Union in a celebrated performance of Handel's *Messiah*. (Photo: Andrew Butterton)

portions of oratorios were given at All Saints' Church with so much delicacy and excellence as deserved the favour with which they were received'. The favoured composer throughout the Choral Union's Victorian experience was undoubtedly George Frideric Handel, whose *Judas Maccabaeus* was given to a 'fashionable and appreciative audience' in early February that year at the Corn Exchange. The conductor was 'Mr Adlington' and the verdict was that it was 'many years since our local musicians gave an equally effective oratorio performance'. By May the chorus had been 'considerably strengthened, both numerically and artistically' for their next venture, Joseph Haydn's *Creation*. For this, local orchestral players were augmented by 'several members of Mr Charles Halle's celebrated band' from Manchester. The Corn Exchange rang to 'grand bursts of harmony' in a 'splendid performance', the product, the *Mercury* declared, of 'the training of such a consummate chorus master as Mr Adlington'. Never again, crowed the paper, would we be 'twitted with the cuckoo-cry that Derby is not a musical town', when the critic found 'the largest hall in town crowded to excess' for a great Viennese classic and scores of people turned away at the doors. There were 230 performers, no less, between band and chorus. In January 1867 it was back to much-loved Handel, this time his *Samson*, heard for the first time ever in Derby. It was 'a great success', and never before, the paper's critic thought, 'have the majesty and power of the Handelian choruses been more steadily or more judiciously indicated'. The orchestra was again fortified with people from London, Leicester, Nottingham and other towns, 'gentlemen who stand in the front rank of their profession'. The basses of the chorus were splendid and the altos too sang well, but 'where we sat the trebles sounded rather weak, and seemed at times almost overpowered'.

Later Victorian choral evenings were at the Drill Hall. It was Handel's *Joshua* in November 1878 with singing of 'great precision and power', and *Messiah* was back in December 1887, filling the house. There was a new music director now, Mr Charles Hancock. The chorus 'sang *con amore* [with love], and the band was a good one'. But for October 1888 there was something new, Dr Stanford's *The Revenge*, to go with the old war-horse *Hymn of Praise* by Mendelssohn and with the accompaniment of no less than the whole illustrious Halle Orchestra conducted by its founder. As for the Derby chorus the *Mercury* had 'never heard it do better'. It was back to Handel in March 1897, combined with the 'Leicester New Musical Society', with a second performance in that town. In December 1900 it was Mendelssohn again, whose oratorio *Elijah* pushed Handel for popularity nationally. The conductor was again Mr Hancock, who directed a 'uniformly good if not tremendous performance'. The work was no doubt chosen deliberately as a crowd-puller as audiences had been dwindling again in recent seasons.

No doubt there would have been plenty of basement vocal back-up for all this artistry in the hundreds of pubs in town, where possibly the largest single tally of leisure hours would have been spent! Pubs were the venues too for the vocal efforts of the various Friendly Societies, where working-class practical solidarity was expressed away from Trade Unions and long before any strong hints of a Welfare State. So in August 1837, on the second anniversary of the 'Derby Rose of Sharon Lodge' of the 'United Ancient Order of Druids' on a Monday afternoon at the Dog and Partridge Inn, after drinking the health of Her (youthful) Majesty 'songs, duets, and glees' helped to fire a meeting which was 'kept up with great spirit till a late hour, when all departed highly pleased with the entertainments in which they had participated'. In May 1856 it was the turn of the 'Derby Midland United Order of Oddfellows' to mark the anniversary of the 'Poor Man's Friend Lodge' at the Griffin's White Hart, Bridge Gate, when the evening was 'enlivened by the presence of the wives and sweethearts of the members, and the cheerful song and merry dance tended to make them forget the toils and cares of life for a while'. Perhaps vocal standards were a little higher back in May 1846 when the 'Harmonic Society' marked the end of their second season with 'a most excellent supper, consisting of every delicacy' at the Green Man Inn, St Peter's Street and 'Messrs Hardy, Drew, Lowe, and others delighted the company by singing a selection of most excellent songs, glees, catches, duets, &c., which added much to the enjoyment of the party'.

Otherwise there was opportunity for Choral Union choristers to exercise their lungs in Sunday church services. Singing on these occasions was, indeed, the subject of critical appraisal in the *Mercury* in March 1878 when there was a correspondence about the efforts at St Werburgh's in particular. The organist there, Mr A.F. Smith, was taken to task by 'An Admirer of a Truly Musical Service' (a lady, apparently) for jettisoning the settings of popular items in *Hymns Ancient and Modern* and substituting his own tunes, which were hardly distinguished by their 'false accentuation and jerky style' that undermined a feeling of devotion. The writer maintained that 'some portions of the music in this church is simply intolerable': the organist 'displays very questionable taste' and 'is evidently no church musician'. Serious stuff! A reply was not long in coming. Why was St Werburgh's 'crowded to overflowing'? Why had the Bishop recently commented on 'the beauty of music' there, an opinion backed by the Dean and Bishop of Lichfield, no less? Mr Smith's degree 'as an

Associate of the College of Organists best shows his qualifications'. But the female critic was backed up by one 'K.G.', who thought St Werburgh's a case of 'a small church with a very so-so choir, and an equally so-so organ atrociously attempting a something in the way of music which it is hopeless for it to achieve with success'.

Operatic interlude

Finally we are back where we started with opera. In early Victorian days the town's taste for it was met by pre-booked seats at Her Majesty's Theatre in London, according to a *Mercury* advertisement by 'Mr Jullien' in April 1846. Considering the cost of travel, even though the Midland Railway was fully up and running by then, this must have been very much a minority taste, as the address to 'the Nobility and Gentry of Derby' surely indicates, with the town's name standing very much in this instance for the county and the target families those in the country seats around. By May 1867 there was no need to travel: at least once a year 'The English Opera Company' was at the Corn Exchange, the opera on that occasion Flotow's ever-tuneful *Martha*, with its stunning song *The last rose of summer*, done by 'the best opera company we have seen in Derby for years'. In later Victorian times it was the turn of the Carl Rosa company, as we have already seen, with the spaces of the Grand Theatre at their disposal. In March 1888 it was the setting for Mozart's ever-popular *The Marriage of Figaro* in its native Italian to a full house, and 'from the opening scene to the *finale* of the last act everything was one continued series of successes, which will long live in the memory of everyone fortunate enough to be present'. And it would soon be Wagner-time!

Visual delights

From 1882 Derbeians had an Art Gallery in which to browse among master paintings of former times. It was built as an extension to the Free Library opened three years earlier through the generosity of Thomas Bass. The basis of the collection that would now be a focus for some of the leisure hours of folk who appreciated art had come from Thorntree House, the recently demolished former home of Bass's predecessor as doer of good works for the town, Joseph Strutt. Some of the pictures have since been downgraded as the work of studio assistants rather than from the hand of a master. But the gallery was one more step in the collective 'good life' of the town. Previously such works would have been the private joy of wealthier individuals, though Strutt had opened up his collection for a small fee on Sunday afternoons in the 1830s. Paintings would be available for purchase from time to time, as in the *Mercury* advertisement by 'R. Moseley' in March 1838. He had some large Joseph Wrights for sale, works 'he has every reason to believe that many persons in the County of Derby have long sought in vain'. He especially mentioned one which 'has been in the possession of Mr Wright's Family to the present time', namely the 'Splendid Picture of the Tomb Scene in Romeo and Juliet' and also one of the Derby master's celebrated 'candle light' paintings, owned by a deceased Liverpool doctor, entitled *Boys Blowing a Bladder*.

By the time the Art Gallery opened it was obvious from *Mercury* reports that a good number of ordinary Derbeians were spending time creating their own canvasses. At the end of March 1878 Richard Keene opened an 'Exhibition of Pictures by Local Artists', presumably in his studio in Iron Gate, in which 'capital bits of local scenery' mingled with the works of

Statue of Thomas Bass beside his gift to the town of the Free Library and Art Gallery, but originally placed in the Market Place in 1884. (Photo: Andrew Butterton)

artists of national repute. *Evening from the Long Bridge, Derby* was singled out by the *Mercury* as 'one of the best things in the collection' and there were 'views of Chaddesden, Dale Abbey, Markeaton Brook, &c.'. These were watercolours but there were also oils by 'deft wielders of the pencil' resident in Derby like J.S. Gresley and George Turner – magic names!

In 1887 the Derby Sketching Club was founded and from 1889 started to hold annual exhibitions, at first in the Athenaeum Rooms. The club rated a 10th anniversary article in the *Mercury* to accompany their 1897 exhibition in the Albert Hall in the Mechanics' Institute in late January. In the early days in the late 1880s members had procured a houseboat at Weston-on-Trent in the summer, ostensibly for sketching and painting in the open air, but who knows what else, judging from the tone of the newspaper account! Derby's best local artists now belonged to the club, so that the latest exhibitions were full of watercolours and oils rather than 'black and white' sketches. That year over 200 works were on show, 89 in oils. Members came from a wide area of southern Derbyshire, like Mr Louis B. Hurt of Alderwasley and Mr George Turner again, of Barrow-on-Trent. Hurt had no fewer than 10 paintings of a 'high standard of merit' on show and his 'On the moorland at Killin' would 'rank as one of the finest paintings in the exhibition'. Hurt did this Scottish genre well, with 'Highland cattle, superbly treated, drinking from a brook'. Turner had 'done so much towards popularising many lovely spots in Derbyshire' and had entered 'one particularly charming painting, "A Ford at Monsal Dale" that included 'a quaint old house by the riverside', plus 'another very attractive work, "Timber clearing at Alderwasley".' There were Italian scenes by Mr William Bemrose. Among watercolours the *Mercury* critic particularly liked Mr James S. Gresley's 'Mill on the Machno, Bettws-y-Coed', leafy little dale, rustic bridge, tiny waterfall and all!

It was the custom in Victorian times for large pictures of especial note to be exhibited on tour on their own, specially mounted behind protective curtains. In early June 1888 Mr

Richard Keene exhibited at his Iron Gate gallery 'Mr Gordon Lewis's great picture of "The Baptism of Christ in Jordan'." The *Mercury* reported that on the previous Saturday he had admitted 'the boys and girls of the Railway Servants' Orphanage' free of charge. By then there was an annual Corporation show at the Art Gallery. The February 1900 show was the 17th and featured several George Turners with mouth-watering titles based on Derbyshire scenery: 'The Way through the Wood, Coxbench', 'A Dell near Kirk Ireton', 'Watering Horses' and 'Windley, Derbyshire' give something of the flavour.

A rival enterprise?

The Victorians pioneered photography and Richard Keene was an early master. He is known as a recorder of the Derby street panorama and for photographic expeditions into the High Peak. In January 1878 he had ready, according to the *Mercury*, 'two volumes of his Derbyshire photography', described as 'the perfection of this class of drawing-room adornment'. He was also responsible for Messrs Clulow and Sons' 'tasteful calendar, which is quite on a par with any we have yet seen'. In May 1888 the paper announced that Keene had 'recently been awarded medals for photographs of Hardwick Hall and Osmaston Manor at Derby, Dublin, Dundee, Gloucester, and the Crystal Palace, in addition to being awarded a certificate at Nottingham'. By September 1897 he had gone on to international honours with a bronze medal at Roanne, France, for 'an interior view of Hardwick Hall'. And another member of the family, M.C. Barrow Keene, had won gold for a photo of 'a Derbyshire Dale'. Back in 1888 there was a Derby Photographic Society in existence. That June they joined forces with the 'Leicester and Loughborough Photographic Society' for a shoot-out at picturesque Wingfield Manor: 'These gentlemen of the camera, possessed of true esprit de corps, formed themselves into one party, and a very pleasant time was spent. Many plates were exposed and excellent pictures taken'.

What choice Derby's Victorians had for their leisure! Indeed from the 1870s there were one or two more. In February 1878 the *Mercury* gave an enthusiastic welcome to 'THE FRIAR-GATE COCOA HOUSE' in contrast to the strong disapproval it meted out in a March issue to another kind of place of recent growth in which to while away the leisure hours, 'WORKING MEN'S CLUBS'. The paper was indignant that the Superintendent of Police and one of his sergeants, after 'effecting an entry... by stratagem', had been unable to do anything about the fact that numbers of people inside one of these premises, address unspecified, were consuming liquor out of hours. They had, 'in spite of the blustering of the proprietor, made some useful observations', which could 'have the effect of opening the eyes of the magistrates'! The situation was not good: 'Any number of people may assemble for the purposes of drinking, gambling, or any other equally reprehensible practices, without the law having any power in the matter, provided the people resorting to the house have paid a nominal fee of say 1s, yearly – and have thus become members of "the club".' These places were 'fitted up in every way like a public-house, with jugs, glasses, and all the facilities for drinking'. The results were 'youths and young women congregate and remain until two or three o'clock in the morning' and 'twenty-five persons are found drinking on a Sunday during the hours when licensed public-houses are closed by law'. So clubbing was alive and well in late-Victorian times!

Iron Gate in about 1859, a photo by Richard Keene showing his studio on the right, safe from the 1860s demolition of the other side of the street. (Courtesy: Derby Museums and Art Gallery)

But it was a different matter with the Cocoa House. It would contribute to the 'vast improvement in temperance' the *Mercury* applauded in May 1897 as shown by statistics published in the same issue to the effect that only six per thousand of Derbeians had been convicted of drunkenness during the previous 12 months. On its opening the paper thought its fortunes 'will be watched with considerable interest'. It could be an answer to:

> ... one of the most perplexing problems of the day. People, especially the working classes, whose homes are, at best, inadequate for the comfort of large families, must have places of resort; and it is absurd to denounce the publican and public-houses, unless superior places are provided.

The 'cocoa place' development was worthy of all support. 'Light, cleanliness, comfort, civility, and really good refreshments are provided at the new establishment. In Liverpool, Hull, Bristol, Newcastle, Birmingham, and Leicester, these cocoa-houses are a great moral and financial success; and we do not think that there is anything exceptional in the circumstances of Derby that should prevent similar results attending the one now open in our midst. A great number of working men appeared to take great interest in the opening ceremony.' And, we hope, women too. They certainly did in Glasgow in the sublime Cranston/Mackintosh tea rooms of the 1890s.

CHAPTER 10

Dying Days

Here in Derby, where the falling snow and the gloomy mist seemed to be specially tuned to the day of mourning, the scene was indescribably solemn. It was a day for the like of which we can remember no parallel – the streets were more silent than on Sundays. There were no tramcars, and scarcely any vehicular traffic. The people were all attired in mourning; the houses had their blinds drawn. The voices were hushed in the streets, and the snow muffled the sounds of the footfalls as the people proceeded to take their part in the ceremony of the day, or wended their way to the various churches and chapels where memorial services were to be held.

(*Derby Mercury*, 6 February 1901)

This was the scene in the county town on the day of Queen Victoria's funeral at St George's Chapel, Windsor, the *Mercury* report capturing the grief-laden atmosphere of the end of an era. She had died at Osborne House on the Isle of Wight at the age of 81 on the previous Tuesday, 29 January, at 6.45pm. The news had reached the Post Office at Derby at the corner of St James's and Victoria Streets at 7.15pm on 'a fine starlit, calm night, and large crowds remained in the streets discussing the event until late. On Wednesday there were universal signs of mourning, many of the shop windows bearing their shutters, the flags being half-masted, and many blinds being drawn.' The Mayor had despatched a message addressed to the Home Secretary at Cowes on the Isle of Wight on behalf of his fellow citizens expressing 'profound sorrow for the loss the nation has suffered by the death of our beloved Queen' and had received a reply from the royal Equerry: 'The Prince of Wales desires me to thank you and the citizens of Derby for the kind expressions of sympathy'. On that Saturday, faintly mirroring the impressive pageant in London when the Queen's body left for Windsor, Derby's 'municipal procession was in itself a memorable one, and was as fully representative as it could be made'. For the last 20 years the town had become a new kind of administrative animal, a County Borough separate from the County of Derbyshire itself. And so on this solemn

The statue of Queen Victoria in front of the DRI, paid for by Sir Alfred Haslam and unveiled by her son King Edward VII on his visit to Derby in June 1906, five years after her death. (Photo: Andrew Butterton)

occasion the High Sheriff of the County, Sir Vauncey Crewe of Calke Abbey, 'wearing the uniform of his office, and accompanied by the retinue of liveried attendants, mostly veterans of the army whose medals testified to the service to their Queen and country', took part together with a 'contingent of mourners' from the separate County Council. The *Mercury* commented: 'thus, for the first time within the memory of many of us, were seen the chief representatives of shire and county town joining together on an occasion of national ceremonial'. It should be added that the County Council's headquarters was still situated inside the borough, in St Mary's Gate.

So Edwardian times had arrived, in fact if not yet in spirit, with the days of transition a time for reflection upon the vast backward-stretching panorama of the Victorian era of nearly 70 years. At the news of the Queen's final illness the *Mercury*'s editor had expressed 'a sense of bewilderment' at the prospect of the loss of the 'only one Monarch all our lives – the beloved Queen'. The paper's edition of 30 January announcing Victoria's death had all seven columns of each of its eight enormous pages edged in black. It was indeed time for looking back as well as trying to peer into the glass of the future darkly.

A broad canvas

The *Mercury* had tried to assess the extent of change on the occasion of the Great Queen's Diamond Jubilee in June 1897. The article was written in general terms, listing the improvements and changes which the country as a whole had experienced during Victoria's reign and which, by implication, the people of Derby had therefore shared to some extent at least. So people drank less at the end of the century than they had in 1837, despite the number of pubs and the number of alcohol-related cases before the Borough Police Court. Women were now much better educated, with high schools for girls and the opportunity of getting to university. They could become doctors and could teach. They filled almost as many clerical jobs as men. People were more sensitive to cruelty. Boys were no longer sent up domestic chimneys and if the fox was still hunted, 'cruelty to animals is tabooed' and there were societies dedicated to preventing or punishing cruelty to children and animals. The idea of what made genuine or healthy sport had changed. While racing had become really popular, almost every middle-class person had 'his or her special form of exercise'. First lawn tennis took over from archery and croquet, but now golf, 'which had swept over the border from Scotland', seemed to be sweeping more southerly boards. There was also the bicycle, 'which in the last two or three years has lifted all classes of society into the saddle'. For the mass of people, cricket and football reigned supreme, the latter for eight months of the year with 'thousands of eager spectators, and the players are the pets and idols of the crowd'. Sunday was not what it was, though in the emphasis on the quietness that prevailed on the day of the Queen's funeral, as we have seen, a comparison was indeed made with normal Sundays. Nevertheless the editor maintained that Sunday had 'become a holiday as well as a holy day'. There were now four more Bank Holidays, most shopkeepers and assistants had half-holidays, the mills closed for a week in the summer and with rail excursions 'only the very poorest in the land are debarred from an annual holiday, however far inland they may live'.

A Boxing Day edition article in 1900 listed the notable buildings which had been added to the Derby scene since 1837, with special emphasis on the growth in hospitals and charitable foundations like 'the Deaf and Dumb Institution, which is handsomely housed in Friar Gate; and the Railway Servants' Orphanage, a splendid home on the Ashbourne Road'. There were also the parks and recreation grounds, which by now through the charitable disposition of 'Mr Mundy, of Markeaton' included one near the northern edge of town in the district known as the West End. Derby people, the writer thought, were 'inclined to be self-deprecatory' but their views had 'fairly kept step with the advancing times'. The town had made good 'use of its opportunities', had been blessed with generous citizens and been governed by careful administrators, which last observation marked a definite change of attitude from the Liberal-bashing the paper indulged in 30 years or so previously.

Life is surely better

The same article ended up telling an imaginary Derby citizen from the early 19th century how good things were now:

Consider! In your day only a few people could read and write. In your day you walked to Nottingham, or you spent 10 hours in getting to London by coach. In ours the Nottingham run takes half-an-hour; we get to London in three, to Paris in a day, to America in a week. Your best idea of a telegraph was a line of signal posts from the sea to London; we have wires and we can communicate with anyone in a few hours; with other wires we can telephone and actually talk to people either in their offices in Derby or their offices in London. Your news from the Continent took weeks to come, now we can get it flashed under the sea, from all parts of the world in a few hours.

You lighted your homes with rushlights or candles; we light our houses or streets with gas or electricity. You took your pitcher to the pump; we get our water, fresh and pure from the country, brought inside our houses. Your bread was dear; ours is cheap. You grew what you ate; we get much of ours over the seas – indeed, we make ice-machines in Derby, which brings meat all the way from Australia. Your only notion of a tram was the old line the father of all the tram-lines in the world, they say, which brought and still brings the coal down from Denby to the canal at Little Eaton; ours is a coach on iron rails, which runs through the principal streets of the town. You probably heard of the hobby horse as a toy, our inventors have turned it into a machine on which our men and maidens career about the country at the rate of 10 miles an hour. You used to think that machinery killed labour; we have discovered that machinery creates labour.

The Derby citizen of 1900, the *Mercury* maintained, was happier, lived longer, had wider interests and keener activities and was healthier. He/she had experienced 'a century of progress for the human race'. There was still a lot to be improved, and a lot that deserved condemnation. The writer could not of course have forseen two appalling world wars and also how the distant countries that supplied his fellow Derbeians with an increasing proportion of their food and goods would eventually provide the town with new creative and productive citizens and a splendid variety of cultures. The multitudinous horrors, the settled confusion, as well as the radio, television, compact disc and unending ordinary conveniences of the 20th century were hidden in the future. The ever-conservative *Mercury* pronounced that religion was now more practical and healthy. Since Derby was the home town of Erasmus Darwin, grandfather of the far more famous and significant Charles, whose book *On the Origin of Species* in 1859 had placed a time-bomb in the world of religious belief, it would be interesting to know how many and how few of its citizens were evolutionists as opposed to holding the common view that the universe was the creation of a Supreme Being. But the firm belief in 1900 appeared to be that things would continue to improve as they had, that Derby belonged to a nation and an Empire in its prime and with the best possible system of government. We now know, a century later, that the dreadfully unexpected was just around the corner! But if we were back in 1900 surely we too would have been confident unless our meagre home were in one of the neglected areas of town. Derby's Victorian experience was the most nourishing in the whole of its long history.

The junction of Victoria Street, the Wardwick, St James's Street and the Strand, which took shape on the completion of the latter in 1879 and before modern alterations permitted to the ground storey presented a harmonious symphony of curving stone, stucco, window frame and decorative ironwork crowning the skyline and still in the author's view the climax of Derby's Victorian townscape experience. (Photo: Andrew Butterton)

Appendix

Extracts from Street Directories:

GLOVER (1849) and KELLY (1903)

* = one business

STREET:	SADLER GATE		IRON GATE		BRIDGE GATE	
YEAR:	1849	1903	1849	1903	1849	1903
accountant				**		
almshouse					*	
architect/surveyor				****		
artists' materials		*				
assurance co.				*		
auctioneer				*		
baker		*				
bank		*		*		
beerseller						*
blacksmith						*
block engraver		*				
boilermaker/engineer					*	*
bones dealer					*	
books				*		
boots/repair/shoemaker	* * *	*	*	*	*	*
brazier	*		*			
brokers					*	
brush manufacture		*				
builder						*
butcher		* * * * *		*		* * *
cabinet maker		*	(& pianos)* *			
carver & guilder	*					
cheese & bacon			*		*	
chemist/druggist	*	*	*	*	*	
china/glass		*		*		
clothing				*		
coach-proprietor	*					
coal-dealer					*	
confectioner	*	* * *	(&tea)*	*		
Convent						*
cookshop			*			

STREET	SADLER GATE		IRON GATE		BRIDGE GATE	
Year	1849	1903	1849	1903	1849	1903
cooper		*				
currier/leather dresser	*				*	*
cutler		*				
cycle & car maker				*		
dining rooms		*				*
draper		*	*	*		
dyer					*	
electrician/locks		*				
farmer		*				
fine art		*				
fish & game		*				(fryer)*
fitter					*	
florist				*		
flour-dealer					*	
french-polisher		*				
fruit					*	
furniture (antique)				*		
furniture remover						*
gardener/seedsman	*				*	
grocer/tea		* * *	*	* *		* * * *
gun-maker		*				
haircutter-perfumer	*				*	
hosiery	*	* *				
inn	* * * *	* * * * *	*	* *	* * * *	* * * *
	(Shakesp.,Horse&J., Half-M.,3Tuns, Bell)		(Rob.H.)	(+wines)	(Gold Lion,Nott.Arm, 3Crowns,Fox&O.,Brit)	
ironmonger				(Bennt's.)*	*	
jeweller/silversmith/ clock & watch	* *	*		(&guns)*		
laboratory			*			
lace-maker			*			
lodgings						*
maltster	*					
marine-stores					*	
milkseller	*					
milliners		*				
model-maker					*	
musical instrum.			(Fould's)*			
music teacher				* *		
machinery (domestic & hortic.)				*		

STREET	SADLER GATE		IRON GATE		BRIDGE GATE	
Year	1849	1903	1849	1903	1849	1903
nail-manufact.					*	
needle-maker					*	
omnibus driver					*	
optician/instr. maker			*			
photographic				*		
plater					*	
plumber		*	(&glaz.)*			*
Presbytery					*	
printers	*		*	*** (&bks+Merc.)		
provisions		*				
railway enquiry off.		*				
restaurant				*		
riveter						*
soda water manuf.					*	
solicitor				*******		
spa ornaments					*	
tailor	*	* * * *		*	*	
taxidermist		*				
tea & coffee				*		
timekeeper		*				
tinplate		*				
tobacco confect.	*				*	
toys				*		
tripe-dresser		*				
veterinary surgeon	*					
weaver					*	
weighing machine					*	
whitesmith (& bell-hanger)					*	

Index